This book is full of little insights that have that Oh yes! quality to them; the world needs more of these writings. It's lovely, I can sense you and hear your voice through your words. It is a joy.
Kris Hughes, Head of the Anglesey Druid Order, Author of *Natural Druidry*

What strikes me the most, when I'm among modern Druids, is their sheer love of life! They are able to express their connection to the land, respect for living things and reverence for the gods in a far richer way than I have been used to as a Priest of another tradition. Yes, like other religions, Druids use ritual and ceremony, but not in a dry and formal way. They have MORE. They have an extra ingredient - ART. Druidry is an artistic belief system that awakens and celebrates creativity with passion and power. It holds together, in perfect balance, both the Priestly and the Bardic dimensions. It is this combination of Priest and Bard that comes across with shining lights in Cat's beautiful book. It is alive, alive with life itself! It is a book written from the heart of a true Priest of nature, with every bit of Bardic magic infused. Covering much new ground, Cat imparts information in a perfectly natural and conversational manner, her poetic imagination making the reading a pure delight.

It is also deeply human. Interspersed are deliciously authentic and highly personal anecdotes that give the book an extra spark of raw humanity. Unlike many modern day spiritual guides and gurus Cat does not attempt to be the archetypal wisdom teacher, sat high upon a throne of perfection. She sits down with us, and opens her heart, sharing both her vulnerability as well as her life-learned lessons. Life can be hard or mundane or confusing, and the Druidry spoken of here is for just such a life. You will find no pie in the sky platitudes, but earthy soul-guidance for real people. Cat paints a picture of a spiritual way of life that stretches, breathes, allows movement and flexibility. Not a religion of perfection and certainties but one that makes sense of life with all its mess and muddle. One that can adapt, embrace and grow.

And not only is this book informative, it is also incredibly practical with pages of time tested and experience gained suggestions on how to bring a dynamic and authentic druidry into one's own life. In the future, when people ask me which book on Drudiry I recommend for someone who really wants to experience what being a Druid means, this will most definitely be among the first that come to mind. I know for certain that it will make enormous sense to all those who have felt that natural inner stirring of nature's magic them, yet have never found the words to name it or express it.

Mark Townsend, Author of *Jesus Through Pagan Eyes* and *The Path of the Blue Raven*

I have stood on a mountain-top in Wales on a freezing dawn after an hour's hard walk, watching the sun rise over the sea and sharing visions.

I have stood in the rain, soaked through, cloak stuck to me and laughing as the wind whips around me, painted with ochre as I dance with the spirits of the forest.

I have sat in the dark, alone, at the bottom of a pit, unsure even of which direction to look next, let alone where to step. – Cat Treadwell, *A Druid's Tale.*

In the American West, in the days of open frontier, there was a character known as the Wagonmaster, whose job it was to gather folks together in the city, and guide them across dangerous, wonderful and uncharted wilderness to a new life in a new world. Pilgrims chose a Wagonmaster not just by what he had to say, but even more so by how he looked and felt. He looked like someone who had spent ages in the wilderness; felt like someone who understood the unknown. In *A Druid's Tale*, Cat Treadwell looks and feels like a spiritual Wagonmaster. She has been there. She has made the journey before. She not only knows how to tell us about it, she knows how to take us in hand and lead us into the wilderness. She is a reliable guide. That is the value of her book. Anyone can write about Druidry, but only a few special folks can take us there. Be prepared for a deep and meaningful journey.

Walter William Melnyk, Author of *Tales of Avalon*, and co-author, with Emma Restall Orr, of *The Apple and the Thorn*

Cat is one of those rare gems. What you see is what you get and what you get is all good. In this her first book she demonstrates very accurately her own view and personal commitment to her path. Typical of her she is a guide and never dogmatic, but certainly worth following. I was fortunate enough to be at her first talk where we rather put her on the spot and she took up the challenge. I was even more fortunate to be at the following years talk where she filled the room. I am even more fortunate to have her as a dear friend.

John Belham-Payne, Co-Founder, The Centre for Pagan Studies

Spun from personal experience, A Druid's Tale is a refreshingly honest, accessible guide to a belief system that is as valid today as it was in ancient times. Non-formulaic, non-exclusive and never preachy, this is an essential read for anyone interested in this vast and fascinating topic.

Russell Whitfield, Author of *Gladiatrix* and *Roma Victrix*

From the spring of new introductory guides to Druidry, this is a book very much written in the informal style of a modern web blog. Warm, bubbly and accessible, it reveals the honest thinking and wakeful self-reflection that should be the foundation of every personal exploration of Druidry – indeed, any belief system – today.

Emma Restall Orr, Founder, The Druid Network, Author of *Living Druidry* and *Living with Honour*

This is a very lively and interesting example of a how it is book of modern spirituality, as opposed to a how to one: and thus one of the best illustrations of how Druidry is lived that I have seen.

Professor Ronald Hutton, University of Bristol, Author of *The Triumph of the Moon* and *Blood and Mistletoe: The History of the Druids in Britain*

A Druid's Tale

An Ancient Path in the Modern World

A Druid's Tale

An Ancient Path in the Modern World

Cat Treadwell

Winchester, UK
Washington, USA

First published by Moon Books, 2012
Moon Books is an imprint of John Hunt Publishing Ltd., Laurel House, Station Approach,
Alresford, Hants, SO24 9JH, UK
office1@o-books.net
www.o-books.com

For distributor details and how to order please visit the 'Ordering' section on our website.

Text copyright: Cat Treadwell 2011

ISBN: 978 1 78099 113 9

A CIP catalogue record for this book is available from the British Library.

Design: Stuart Davies

Printed in the USA by Edwards Brothers Malloy

We operate a distinctive and ethical publishing philosophy in all
areas of our business, from our global network of authors to
production and worldwide distribution.

CONTENTS

For Jim
The best of men and the keeper of my heart
and Cafall
The wisest and most loyal of guard dogs

'What a blessing it is to love books as I love them, to be able to converse with the dead, and to live amidst the unreal.'
Thomas Babington Macaulay

'Blessed are the cracked, for they shall let in the light.'
Groucho Marx

Acknowledgements

Since I first learned to read, I've had a core dream of writing a book myself, which I bored English teachers with throughout my schooldays. Many of them won't ever read these words, but for all those teachers and friends who encouraged me and do see this – thank you. I wouldn't be here without your kind words.

To Fox and Robyn. For kicking me repeatedly, dragging me out into public view (occasionally at spear-point), and then supporting me so wonderfully when it was most needed. And for telling me that I had a sexy voice on the radio.

To Alex, Morna and Jack. For honouring me more than I can ever express with that first handfasting request. I hold the memory of your day, always.

To my teachers, Bobcat and Verruca Moonbeam! Soul-deep thanks.

And to those whom I studied alongside, those fellow Living Druids and ADO lovelies – for all that wisdom and laughter.

To my fellow Trustees of The Druid Network: Nessa, Bish, Red, Chris and Phil (and families). Hard workers, dear friends, whose value to me truly is beyond price.

To Jamie Magpie and the original Apple Grove, for those first steps (with Prince Lump and the moving trees!).

To Andy and Sally, for capturing dreams.

To my students, those I have married, and those who have sought me out with bravery and curiosity. I cannot adequately express my thanks.

To those who've supported me in spirit through this amazing and mad journey. Know that you truly *are* honoured, daily.

To those writers it has been my pleasure to know, and for your invaluable advice. Especially useful when the going's been tough.

To Mum, Dad, David and the (growing) family, for putting up with me. And, of course, Fen and Harry, for the unconditional love.

Foreword

The difference between hearing and listening is vast. Generally we hear much and listen little, selecting the information that we deem useful, needful or enriching and dismissing that which serves no obvious purpose. In the process, we may become victims of the forgetfulness of life and succumb to mediocrity and apathy, afraid to listen to the rhythm of magic and inspiration that sings at the core of our being. To some, the voice of the spirit will sing so loudly one cannot help but listen - and then what? What do we do with that calling, how do we respond to the voice of mystery? We start by listening.

Books will call us to ponder over words in the hope of direction, clarity and inspiration. For a writer to be effective, her intent must be rooted in honesty, vulnerability and truth. By laying bare the bones of her Druidry, by opening her veins to the intoxicating streams of Awen that lie within them, Cat causes one to stop and listen. There is much wisdom in the pages that follow, a wisdom far older than the years of the author, a deeper kind of magic that rises from the spirit of a priest who has learnt to listen with intent, humility and strength. From this listening, we are introduced to Druidry of the heart.

What is Druidry? I have heard that question uttered a thousand times or more. This book is different, in that it seeks not to answer that question, but instead to address something far more fundamental and profound: *why* is Druidry? Cat embarks on a journey that seeks not to tell us what Druidry is, what to do or how to do it. Instead, she explains *why* - why she does it - and this is unique. There is vulnerability here; we can empathise with the journey and identify facets of ourselves within it. The majority of authors write of what they know. Very rarely does one encounter an author who writes of *why* they know. This is a book of whys.

Imagine a deep valley. At its centre stands a wood of ancient trees. Drums beat from within, lights flicker in its groves. A circle of people surround the woodland. You stumble from the valley's steep sides to approach them in search of your path, to the sanctuary of the forest. From the myriad individuals who separate you from the trees, a figure approaches, her smile reassuring. The grazes upon her knees are a sign of her own struggles down the mountainside. She takes your arm and leads you towards the trees, whispering of her journey. Her words are familiar and you are guided by her experience to the woodland edge. With tears, a smile and a reassuring hug, she sends you well-equipped into the forest of Druidry to live the tradition of sages.

I've known Cat for several years and have been privileged to share moments of magic and deep transformation in her company. I watched a young Cat grow into the priest she is today, a girl transformed into a woman who lives her Druidry. This book is an account of her path and the challenges it presented to her, challenges that will be familiar to you. It is an account of a growing Druidry, of a living tradition that sings from the land to rise through root and tree, through blood and sap to inspire those who chose to listen to the wondrous peals of Awen that sing of the origination of the soul.

Why do Druids do what they do? Read on: allow the wisdom and experience of one who has delved into the beating heart of Druidry to inspire your own journey into the dappled groves of an ancient tradition.

Kristoffer Hughes
Author and Head of the Anglesey Druid Order
Isle of Anglesey, January 2012

The First Step

The sun is about to rise. We can all feel it, almost tangible, a faint glow in the sky, the first birdsong, the wind picking up as if in welcome. The world holds its breath...

I step into the stone circle. Bare feet tread firmly onto dew-damp grass, toes digging into the earth. I hold my warm cloak tightly closed – dawn in England is a chill time, even in summer. I taste the fresh air in my lungs, in my throat, on my lips. I suppress the urge to laugh that bubbles up inside. Soon. Things to do first.

I'm aware of those around, taking their own steps, walking their own path around the ancient monoliths. How many have come here before us, at this time, for this purpose? No way of telling – unless we know how to truly listen, to hear their stories; as we learn how to tell our own.

I find my place, planting my feet, feeling my roots slide deep into the rich soil. Fingers tingle as I reach out, feeling my companions as they connect with the land. The sea breeze brushes through my hair, the golden glow of first light illuminating everything from here to the horizon.

We open our souls and sing to the dawn, on that mountaintop at the end of the world.

When the laugh comes, it is with pure joy. And I am not alone.

Introduction

To begin with, that most asked question:

'But what IS Druidry?'

Otherwise known as 'Why Do You Do That?'

I'd been a practising Pagan for over ten years, working quietly by myself, occasionally with groups, but generally learning in my own way. Until the time seemed right to undertake actual structured training in the Druid path, culminating in the decision to act rather more publicly to help others when needed, to work more openly, and generally talk about what I did if called upon.

I was then asked to give a talk on Druidry at a national Pagan event, with five minutes' notice, due to someone else not arriving, for an audience of about 20 people. It went well enough that they asked me back the following year... to an audience of several dozen.

In an effort to actually structure something a little more coherent, I decided to start an online blog, in order to ask the world what it is that they actually wanted to *know* about Druids.

Not only am I still writing, my words are now brought together in this book.

From tiny acorns...

We are fortunate, in this time of worldwide information. There are any number of books explaining what Druidry is, from historical accounts by classical authors to 'how to' books by contemporary writers. A quick glance at the internet will provide a wealth of information (a good deal of it contradictory).

I think it is fair to say that what follows can only ever be Druidry According to Me. Which is not to say that mine is the only way – far from it. But it is my *perspective*, which I will explain in due course. I can do no more. Clearly it strikes a chord with people, otherwise I wouldn't be here writing about it, nor be asked to go out in public and talk about it! I also thank you for your interest, and trust that my words kindle a spark of inspiration in you too.

However, I think it is also true that the question is not 'What IS Druidry', but more 'What Do Druids Do?' Well, I can tell you what *I* do, and how this comes under the heading of Druidry... and then it's up to you what you do with it. How does that sound?

How to Read This Book

Personally, I would recommend that these pages be consumed slowly and with consideration, in small bites. You are, of course, quite welcome to race through the whole thing, consuming it entirely in one go. But there's a lot to digest. Perhaps one chapter at a time, with space taken between to really think about what's been said and how it relates to you.

I cannot predict what you take from it, but hope that you enjoy the tales, and are each inspired by my stories as you move on with your own. I have read of the ancient Druid practices, in words written by Roman historians years afterwards. How they advised great leaders and kings, learned and taught, divined the future and told stories of the past. How they fought screaming against the destruction of their groves on the shores of Mona (modern-day Anglesey).

I have read of modern Druids, in the UK, Canada, America and Australia. How they meet to revive the traditions of their ancestors, whether real or imagined, feeling once again their connection to the land.

I have read of fictional Druids. Of their magic, their golden sickles, their power.

The tales are told to remind us, to inspire us, to fire our imaginations. As we tell them, so do we live them.

I have stood on a mountain top in Wales on a freezing dawn after an hour's hard walk, watching the sun rise over the sea and sharing visions.

I have stood in the rain, soaked through, cloak stuck to me and laughing as the wind whips around me, painted with ochre as I dance with the spirits of the forest.

I have sat in the dark, alone, at the bottom of a pit, unsure even of which direction to look next, let alone where to step.

The tales are told to mark times of change, to remind us of what is important, to explain the unexplainable.

I have stood in a circle of expectant families, both of blood and soul, witnessing the joining of two people on one of the most important days of their lives. I am responsible for holding that energy, the concerns, fears and joys. I must then explain it to those for whom it is new, who had forgotten their connection, who need words to describe what they just felt.

I have spoken on national radio via telephone, an hour before a major ritual, from the normality of my kitchen and yet with the otherworldliness of burning incense and robes. I try to imagine who might be listening – and who I represent.

I have been pulled into giving a talk on Druidry with five minutes' notice, trying to speak my truth honestly and create understanding in a room full of strangers, while forcing myself to forget the all-encompassing phobia of public speaking from my schooldays.

I made a promise to walk the path of a Druid Priest, when I held sufficient tales that I must pass them on to others in order to keep them alive.

I have been called upon, and I have answered.

I am still learning, and will be throughout my life. I can never predict what I will be asked to do next, but know to take a deep breath and step forward – I will be caught and held. I remind myself of this when alone and needing solace (sometimes in the most crowded of places).

Modern Druidry is connection, relationship, to each other and to the greater world (both seen and unseen). It is responsibility for yourself and others, human and non-human, with a view to gaining a greater understanding of our place and what we are doing in this life. And while intrinsically alone, we are never truly isolated – there is always someone there with us.

That's a start.

Titles

'So what's a Druid?'
This question is generally danced around, in these days of political correctness. But it hangs in the air between the smartly-dressed 'normal' person and the woman in robes, staff in hand, adorned with leaves.

I consider myself very fortunate to live in these times, when I can live my spirituality openly and not be castigated, criticised or driven out of my community. In fact, I've found that most people are curious enough to approach and ask questions, once they see my smile and know that it's OK. Conversation and discussion all help understanding and, once the common ground is found, there's very little negativity (the occasional joke about golden sickles and henges notwithstanding).

Everyone has an ingrained urge to question, never really able to shake off their childish curiosity about that which they do not understand (and there's quite a lot of that in the world). We're all humans, walking our path and striving to do our best, within our understanding, with what we are told and what we learn for ourselves along the way. Without some level of seeking, we remain closed, cut off from everything around, unable to fully participate or connect – unable to really live.

Unfortunately, the downside to this secular, modern world is that it is difficult to construct the appropriate language in which to question, to frame sincere and honest curiosity correctly and yet remain polite. But overcoming fear of the unknown is a great strength, and I'm glad that so many take that leap in simply taking an interest.

I prefer the straightforward approach.

'How can you call yourself a Druid?'
It was my decision to do so – essentially, to label myself. The

easiest answer is that 'Druid' is the word that describes most easily what I do, quick shorthand that aids understanding when a long explanation won't be heard. Everybody has an idea of what a Druid is. The next common question involves white robes (and my own lack of).

The Druids were, and are, the priests of this land, my homeland by birth. Everywhere has its indigenous priests, the shamans and wild folk, those who work more deeply with the seasons and the spirits than most everyday folk. The Druids were those of the British Isles.

Modern Paganism is the fastest-growing spiritual path of the twenty-first century, as people seek meaning from the actions of their ancestors and relationship with the living world around them. Philosophy, Religion and Science have not solved the mysteries of human living – but these join together in the Druid, the teacher and seeker, leading the way between the known and unknown.

I claimed the responsibility and duties of this title before my Gods as part of my promise, as Awenydd (Priest), one storm-tossed night on Anglesey, and am reminded of it often. Every time I stand up to take my place as officiant at a public rite; when simply speaking quietly to advise a patient who is lost and afraid, in the ovatic green work uniform that I used to wear; even just in my everyday life.

Who sees the connections, the web between us all, in these cynical post-modern times? Walking the fine line between empirical reality and subjective otherworldliness, a line so sharp that if you step the wrong way, madness follows. But which is preferable – the madness of seeing too clearly the enormity of it all, or the far more acceptable insanity of ultra-normality?

Once the promise is made to truly *see*, to be aware, awake and responsible, there is no turning back. Nor would I want to.

Simply put, I bear witness as part of my connection to the wider universe of which I am a tiny part. To the turning of the year, the changing times, relationships held and lost, times of darkness and light. The difference in energy between night and day, laughter and anger, wakefulness and sleep. Truth and falsehood.

I promised to walk my Truth as best I can and, of course, it isn't easy. It means I cannot simply overlook wrongness for the sake of simplicity and a quiet life – from the crying woman alone on a street corner, to the sale of meat so far removed from its original state that it can scarcely be called food.

If modern priests (both pagan and of all faiths) do not help those who need it, whether immediately in front of us or far away, then who will? Who is there to listen, to see, to hold a hand that has absolutely nobody else in the world? To get dirty and messy in those bloody and screaming times when far more rational folk turn the other way and walk by, scared to even look for fear of what they may see?

I don't claim to be perfect, nor is my life full of sweetness, ease and Enlightenment. I don't think it could be, not while remaining real. I fall down as much as the next person – but each time, I try to learn, to take that pain and carry its tale with me, so I see it better in others and understand.

My Druidry is my life and my work, my joy and my darkness. I walk my path, moving forward with my eyes open. I cannot turn back.

Questions

Prior to a talk that I was giving on Druidry at a national convention, I asked for questions from friends (both pagan and not). I include some of the responses here.

I love being asked questions – you never know what folk will ask. Such discussion also helps enormously in questioning *myself*, ensuring that I really *do* believe what I'm saying... and if I don't, how best to elaborate on feelings and experiences that are often very difficult to describe.

'Can you see Druidry as a mass religion of the future, and do you think that shamanic practices will help society to be less self-centred?'
In a word – no. It never was, and I don't think it ever will be a mass anything. There are always going to be those who want to stand forward as well as those happier to sit quietly; that's all part of the variety of Us! But to link to another two questions (which have been pinging around in my head all day because they're rather good):

'What improvements can Druidry bring to society that cannot be accomplished by other means? Given its broad encompassing of all and any beliefs, what can Druidry provide that differs from other faiths?'
I think the very fact that Druidry is becoming more nationally (and internationally) recognised as a valid faith/mode of thought/way of life rather than just another fringe group speaks volumes about how it *is* needed in the world today. Certainly in England – I receive calls from folk shyly and nervously asking for help with something they want, but don't really know how to ask for, because there *is* no other 'service' that does what Druidry does. The fact that it is so all-encompassing – i.e. all things to all people, rather than evangelical – makes it very approachable, more so perhaps than some of the other occult or mystery traditions.

That's not at all an attempt to undermine other faiths – everyone can call their chosen consultant to ask for advice in life, whether professionally or personally. It is clear, however, that certain individuals are stepping up now and openly asking questions, not necessarily for pat answers (although the self-help books show they're out there too, inevitably), but for ways to genuinely help themselves as responsible players in a wider community. In that sense, yes: Druidry is helping to make society less self-centred. People are interested in involving themselves in life rather than sitting passively by, and that's good.

As Druidry is a shamanic path, it is important to realise what shamanism truly is (rather than just another 'quick fix' buzz-word in a New Age marketing campaign). Put very simply, shamans work with multiple levels of reality to heal, to serve their communities. In that sense, Druidry is absolutely a shamanic tradition, and those who practise Druidry would do well to learn shamanic skills.

However, the difference between a specific Druid or shaman Priest and a simple practitioner can be wide, and misunderstood. No pagan skill set will solve every problem in life, not individually or societally, no matter what some books may say. Any faith that claims to do so is heading dangerously down the path of religious egotism.

But having a wider understanding of the universe as learned through these skills, when carefully and consciously applied, *will* have an impact on your life and the wider world, even if simply by the realisation that you are part of a greater whole. Many faiths offer this, not just shamanism. Whatever calls to you as a path of understanding is worth exploring.

As we are now seeing, the current way of life in the Western world has reached snapping point as we realise how limited it is. Nothing provides all the answers, but there are (finally) ways of thinking that provide a bit of guidance with getting through, and the tools to help with the battle we all engage in daily, called Life. Other faiths are waking up to that, of course, but it's a question of how relevant people feel certain paths are. If nobody walks them, they fade. Paganism as a whole is growing rapidly. I'd go so far as to say that, due to its challenging nature, Druidry has greater potential long-term than others, due to this growing acceptance but also its immense practicality and application.

'Given that modern druidry is a religion based on a pre-Christian belief system, why is there any separation between modern Druidry and modern paganism?'

In a nutshell, paganism is the overarching term; Druidry is

one of the branches. Is it a religion?

'Isn't it just an excuse to get drunk, take drugs and have orgies all under the banner of it being a legitimate religion?'
I would question whether it's a religion at all. A spirituality, a faith and a way of thinking/viewing the world, yes, but Druidry does not espouse certain views to the exclusion of others, and has no central dogmatic text. There are so many different types of Druid (including Christian) that it has become something entirely new – which is why it's incredibly hard to categorise, pin down and stick in a box.

I'm not going to go through all the 'what Druidry is/not' arguments here – that's easily found on the internet and in most bookshops.

And I've never taken drugs or had orgies in the name of Druidry. Sorry about that. Drinking as a celebratory act is entirely different!

'How can you claim Druidry is not a religion whilst also claiming that it is 'a faith and way of thinking/viewing the world' considering that the Cambridge dictionary defines religion as 'the belief in and worship of a god or gods, or any such system of belief and worship'?'
Right. First off, I didn't claim that Druidry wasn't a religion (and I didn't mention gods). I said that *I* would question whether it is a religion; religion as taken to mean a set mode of belief, as dictated by dogma (set text) and espoused by a guru/s of whatever sort. Which is why I'm one of those who does not follow the 'it's the Old Religion of the British Isles, how dare you persecute it because age makes it more valid' argument.

But I actually quite like that Cambridge definition. I do believe in deity, but in the same way that I believe I have a head on my shoulders – not because I was told to, but because of personal experience based on a certain spiritual understanding. I don't think anyone's experience of their gods can be lumped with anyone else's; it's far too personal, unique to the individual. Does that make everyone their own religion, perhaps?

As a brief aside, what about the line between 'religion' and 'cult'? I've heard Nottingham referred to as a 'heathen city' because of the multitude of faiths practised there! But that's a whole different discussion, for another day.

Anyway, to elaborate:

'Has the term 'Druidry' become such a broad term that it is rendered meaningless as a description of spiritual practice?'

While the label of *Druidry* may mean subtly different things to different people, that doesn't so much make it meaningless, but it does inevitably set up certain expectations. Which is why, in saying that while it's not a religion it *is* a faith or spiritual practice, it's very hard to understand under our current default interpretation of 'religion' as a term. Again, language is ill-equipped to describe the details of a very experiential practice. Druidry is not just an intellectual exercise – you have to *do* it to understand it.

When I call myself a Druid, it's on the understanding of Druid as a Priest of the land. Not *worshipping* the land (as a graven idol, say), but seeing the sacred in the land, and our lives as part of that relationship, as any other living thing here.

Once other people gain some understanding of this, it's then up to me to tailor those expectations based on my actions and explanation (as I'm trying to do). Nature is not my god/dess – it's something he/she is part of, as are we all.

Personally, I do agree that the labels we give ourselves are largely to please the wider community. Those on the inside of the Pagan world have read so many books and seen so many definitions, any label is probably meaningless due to being far removed from what it originally was meant to be. The example above of 'Heathen Nottingham' is good – I'd never have said that, but my understanding of the term 'heathen' is very different to the speaker (a Christian priest, ironically!)... but understanding was there, as we comprehend what was meant. So no problem.

As others have said, I think that if Druidry ever has to pin down and classify what it *really is* for the sake of auditing purposes (e.g. the Census, national faith recognition or similar), there will come the difficulties. No set definition: some say religion, some don't, no one leader, no Big Book of Truth. It's a tough issue, which I'm sure won't be answered to everyone's satisfaction.

Ultimately, so long as understanding is achieved, do the intricacies of definition matter?

'How did you actually find your path?'
and
'How do you get to 15th level and become the Hierophant of the Cabal? And what's the recipe to Getafix's magic potion?'
Ahem.

It's easy to find out about Druidry. Go onto any search engine and look it up. You'll find out lots. Some of it conflicts. Some of it is rubbish, fantasy or straight fiction. Such is diversity of belief. (You can probably find out about the 15th level question too, but why on earth you'd *want* to be that is beyond me!)

Lots of people ask how I *know* I'm a Druid, how I 'do' it. That's fine – after all, Druidry is an experiential, lived spirituality. But I would say, how do you know you're *whatever* it is that you call yourself? For example:

I know I'm a public services worker because that's what I do.
I know I'm a writer because that's what I do.
I know I'm a Druid because that's what I do.
With me?

I don't know if I ever 'found' this path, as a sudden realisation. I found out about Druidry via word of mouth among the pagan community, after finding that through reading books and investigating various websites. Eventually, I thought 'oh, that's what you'd call it' – I've been outside talking to trees and things that other people couldn't see since as far back as I can remember. The name for that didn't really matter when I was five years old (and no, I'm reliably informed it wasn't insanity!).

One thing I think I have overlooked here that is so crucial to my Druidry, I took it as read that you'd all understand is *inspiration*. Druidry is the term for what inspires me in life, which is certainly a vital component of what it is people seem to be seeking these days, and hard to find in these cynical times.

Inspiration is key to Druidry. Beautifully told in the story of Cerridwen, whose cauldron spilt the Awen (inspiration) for the Druid Taliesin, it's most commonly depicted these days as three drops, with three rays of light shining from them. Or, in modern cartoons, as a light bulb above the head – the 'aha!' moment of connection, realisation and urge to *do*, to create from within yourself.

To take a handy metaphor, the magic potion that makes you strong contains whatever *you* put into it. Whatever keeps you going, fuels the fire that makes your heart beat fast, puts a smile on your face and allows you to move forward. You cannot see the light bulb above your head if your eyes are shut, or if you're stuck in the dark. You have to reach for it. You have to *do* it, really live, deeply and actively. It's not easy, but nothing worth having ever is.

To keep with that wonderful Getafix idea, yes – I know the cauldron, that deep, dark place of potentiality. I can show it to you. But it's up to you to take a sip from what's inside, if that's what you want.

Druidry *is* a mystery tradition. Metaphor and story are the teachers of experience. But behind the words there is history, tangible, lived reality, solidity and foundation... otherwise I wouldn't really have much to stand on, would I?

How do you find your path? Look outside. It's that stone thing, leads to the garden gate. And beyond that, who knows?

Lots to see on the way though. Step forward with me.

Discovery and Deity

Another lovely question:

*'[Discuss] The decisions people make when they discover Druidism...
do you hang on to the bits of your existing faith that you like, or must
it be a once and forever adoption of the new?'*

Obviously this is pretty subjective to each individual but, first
of all, one thing Druidry *isn't* is dogmatic. There is no 'must', no
dogma or doctrine that you must follow or you're not 'a proper
Druid'. And we're not a cult – it's lovely to have you here, but
there's no demand to renounce any previous beliefs forever, with
no chance of escape!

Personally, I think it's fair to presume that in life, each person
is the sum of their experiences. Nothing is truly thrown out and
forgotten, although things can be left behind if they're no longer
relevant (for whatever reason, whether by choice or circum-
stance). Spirituality and method of worship are among the most
personal life-choices that you can make, so they must continually
be questioned and tweaked to remain an active part of everyday
life – otherwise, why are you following that path if it diverges
from your own experience so much?

Whatever you were brought up with as a child may no longer
ring true to you as an adult, but it's still something held within
you as an experience that resonates. If Catholic ritual with its
altar, cup and incense feels particularly sacred to you, it's likely
you'll follow a mode of practice as a pagan that utilises similar
methods. If you're uncomfortable with such trappings and prefer
to speak to deity directly, you'll be best out in the wild, with the
trees as your church and the birds as congregation.

Changing faith is not necessarily an easy transition, but
sometimes it has to be done. Relationships change, including
your own with your understanding of the world and how you

work within it. Do you cast off everything you knew before, or do you step gently into something new, bringing your own experiences with you?

One thing Druidry *does* do is encourage you to face your fears. Don't be afraid of change. Your spirituality is what you make it – that lack of dogma allows tremendous freedom, which is daunting for many. But take your courage, get out there and see what works best for you. Explore, be curious and watch your faith evolve as you do, and the world around as that connection is continuously forged and maintained.

'[Can] one be a Druid (or indeed any named faith) without including deity worship? Or straddle two belief systems, such as Druidism and Buddhism. What would/do you think of someone who professed to be a Druid but didn't take part in the ritual/deity side of the faith?'

This has been an issue long-discussed in pagan media, notably those who choose to be Christian Druids. As above, your faith is what you make it, but this also includes the question of how you view deity. What is your relationship with Him/Her?

A crucial tenet of Druidry is being aware of the sacredness in Nature – essentially everything around you in the world, *including you.* Deity is not a supernatural force on high, external to the universe – it is present within it, in every breath, every sunrise.

While this may seem to conflict with other faiths, I don't actually see any problem with the idea of deity as fully present in Creation. Without wishing to particularly pinpoint any of the other major religions, I believe that most of them encourage respect of the Earth and everything living within and on it. It's simply extending that a little to include your relationship with the world as being *part* of it, rather than as a caretaker, or someone who simply uses what it provides as if the Earth were a resource of infinite capacity. There are more similarities between faiths than may be apparent at first glance, but I think the misunderstandings largely stem from the 'fire and brimstone' aspects getting more press than the 'peace and love' aspects.

Therefore, following the foundation tenet of Nature as sacred, I don't think it's possible to not take part in the ritualising/deity aspects of Druidry. Every time you step outside and feel the connection to the earth, you're connecting to spirit. Lighting a candle (on a birthday cake?) is a ritual. Dressing to express yourself is a ritual of self-love. You don't need to cast a circle and make proper obeisance to be an active Pagan, of whatever path.

One of the wisest things I ever read about spell-work (I forget where, sadly) is that ritual begins from the first moment that you begin considering it. From that point on, during the time spent compiling bits and pieces to include, formulating words to say, and then finally bringing it all together in the rite itself – that is *all part of the work.* Your intention is formed and off you go. From that spark, the gods are paying attention. So make it good, whatever you're doing.

There's been a lot written about the purposes of ritual, what should and shouldn't be done. Part of me thinks this is harking back to the dogmatism of the mainstream faiths, with well-established traditions set up for a reason; partly it seems to be more Disney-magic – if you say the wrong word or misspell a rune, the brooms will be dancing around the kitchen!

I've taken part in 'play' ritual. In a fantasy setting, celebrating the spirit of Spring coming back to the land with lots of people in costume, lots of paraphernalia and flowers, and a lovely lass representing 'Lady Spring' appearing and thanking us all as she danced about. I was nervous initially, but kept in mind that it was essentially 'play', and threw myself in.

Afterwards, several people approached me with strange looks on their faces, with comments such as "You've done this before, haven't you?" Yes, in fact – two days ago, at Beltane. Throughout the play-rite, the smile would *not* get off my face, due mostly to the sound of my own Lady laughing herself into a fit behind me!

My Goddess was present and highly amused – and understood fully what was going on. While I was left wondering if it was actually possible to even play without putting even a little intention into your words.

We can be Druids quietly, in our homes, to ourselves. We can work publicly helping others, as true Priests. But we are constantly within our sacred space, living our spirituality as best we can. Anyone who takes up the challenge deserves respect, and I find myself more curious about methods than questioning their reasoning.

On this small page, I perform a tiny ritual and call hail – to the Lord and Lady of Spring, so close we can see their fingertips in the daffodil buds and sunny blue skies. Our hearts lift as we ready ourselves to set forth on the work of this season. Let's see what we're called upon to do.

Living and Learning

One thing I've always found missing from the pagan 'How To' books (and believe me, I've seen a fair few) is how to really live as a pagan day-to-day. Then I was asked this too, in public... which made me realise why it isn't in the books. It's a hard question.

A lovely little book I've held on to is called 'Everyday Magic'[1] – lots of mini-spells and rhymes for every conceivable daily occurrence. Pretty, and nice when making presents for people. But aside from the 'witches' on television, who goes through life doing spells every second of the day?

I'm not going to define 'magic' for the umpteenth time. Chances are, if you're reading this, you'll have your own thoughts on it already. It seems to be more a question of how to live as a pagan (Druid/Heathen/Wiccan/etc) in a truly spiritual manner. While retaining reality and not annoying the heck out of everyone around you (no, it is NOT a requisite of my faith to carry an athame/wand/bag of crystals at all times).

The first thing the books always teach is How to Ground. I was lately asked 'WHY do this?' Simple: it's *so you don't fall over.* When working magic, astrally projecting or even just going to the shops, the ground is always there. It's the Thing That Holds You Up. No escaping it. Try not to overdo your daily energy quota (working) without recharging (resting, taking nourishment), because you'll collapse. Fact of life.

And that *is* the first lesson in living as a Pagan, of whatever path. No matter how many 'spells' you do to batter life into the shape you want, mundane reality is always there when you get back. The trick in then living is to realise where the two worlds meet, quite literally.

The places where you need magic in life most are the places where it is hardest to find. Stuck at a desk, in the middle of a city, on the hottest day of the year, with too many demands on your time. So, are you grounded? You'd deal better if you were. Movies might suggest jumping into Narnia, but why bother? Bring Narnia to you. It was created in this world, after all. By a person at a desk.

The universe is magic.

Yes, it's hard. So practise. If your boss is haranguing you, you're frazzled, people are shouting – but if you take a single second to just root down and remember *who you are*, what's important to *you*... you'll be solidly placed to take the next step.

That was a spell, right there. You changed your perceptions and so your life, just a little.

I once asked in a public forum whether Druidry wasn't actually a constant quest to connect more to the Awen, to be inspired every second of your life. To maintain that connection to the universe, to better really *live*. The response was mixed, to say the least. Generally the question was disregarded as that of a naive newcomer.

I still stand by it, though. While I realise you can't be in ritual head-space every second of the day (unless you like white jackets with really long arms), the connection is always there. You block yourself off as a survival mechanism due to the sheer BUSY-ness of today – I know, I've done it often. But when you just take time – even that single *second* – to stand and rejoin the *real* real world, above and beside the mundane... you remember why you do this. The gods are all around us, it's up to us to open our eyes and look.

And really live your connection.

Lunchtime in London. The streets swarm with people, hurrying from offices to cafés, grabbing a sandwich and then returning to their desks. Mobile telephone conversations continue while food is ordered and paid for. Everyone is thinking twenty things at once. Nobody is truly focusing. Each person might as well be alone, for all the attention they pay to anyone – or anything – else.

I'm taking a break today, actually leaving the office for once. I'm furious. A bad morning, nothing's gone right, the boss is angry. I've done my best, and it wasn't good enough. But I know I did my best. Impotent frustration makes me charge down the street like a woman on a mission, fingers clenched into fists, glaring at those who dare to stand in my way. My rage parts the oblivious commuter stream like waves.

On the bridge, I stop, breathing hard. The sky is grey, the skyline familiar. St Paul's Cathedral. Tower Bridge. Scaffolding holding the skeleton of the latest tower block. Modern and antique, sharing space. Through it all runs the river. I stand above it, looking down. Grey-blue and implacable, like the storm-flecked sky above, like my mood.

"Fine," I whisper, not caring who's listening. "Come on, then. Show me, London. I'm here. I want to see what's really going on."

There's got to be more to life in the city than this stupid rat-race, and I want to see it.

The wind picks up, blowing a sudden gale through my hair. And there she is.

Huge. Ancient. The Thames like an artery, flowing through the living land and out to the distant sea. So many steps have been walked in this place, stories told, blood spilt, lives lived.

I can feel it. All of it.

I gasp, unable to breathe.

And then I'm just me again, standing on a fragile Georgian bridge in the twenty-first century.

I inhale, tasting it – the traffic fumes, faint salt on the air, refuse, cooking food. I feel the history passing through, the living energy of the city on my fingertips, in my blood.

I know. I asked, and I was heard.

I bow slightly, smiling my thanks, and return to the office, carrying some of that energy with me. I can't stop smiling for the rest of the day.

The act of 'grounding' is often spoken of in modern spiritual practice as an introductory exercise, and is fairly important as Foundation Level Paganism. But, as with a lot of such work, folk are often shown how to 'ground', but not given much explanation. Why do we *need* to do this? What does it do?

(Don't panic, I'll explain the terminology. Bear with me.)

I have to smile when I hear stories of this. It sums up a lot of the 'how to' books out there, in that pagan learners of any path tend to be *told* what to do, but not necessarily why. We find out as we bimble along, making learner mistakes and bouncing back to exercises that help (once we realise why we were taught them in the first place), but I agree – I'd quite like to know why I'm doing something as I go along.

Pagans – be they witches, druids, heathens, etc. – don't just believe or act out their faith, they *practise* too. And practise, as we know, is continuous (to make perfect, naturally). A big foundation of that work is based on energy. Not to teach your grandma to inhale ovulations, but a lot of 'magic' is energy manipulation… which means that grounding is necessary.

Grounding is basically taking the energy you've worked with or raised, and settling it back down again, bringing yourself back to reality and not remaining in a small, hyperactive, bouncing bubble that burns out very quickly. Imagine a puppy on Red Bull. Follow this through to its logical conclusion. The crash is not pretty, and neither is the mess left in its wake.

Raising Energy is something we all do, magic or not. Runners generate a lot of energy, for example. So do actors and performers. You know the energized feeling when you're about to go on-stage – and that same buoyancy when you step off again afterwards? Whether you enjoyed the experience or not, that's energy.

The classic training step to prove that energy even exists is to rub your hands together fast, generating enough static that you can feel it when you pull your hands apart, like electricity zapping between your palms.

Taking on too much energy, or holding onto it with no release, is bad no matter how you do it. It goes to your head quickly and, while you are capable of accomplishing a fair bit, it may not necessarily be of any quality (you know the feeling of nervous energy?). You will quickly burn out, with a huge pressure headache and possible physical collapse.

The best exercise for raising and grounding your energy in pagan work (or at all) is to plant your feet squarely on the floor, feeling yourself fully *present*, there and then, solid and firm in foundation. Barefoot is good, but not essential – your toes can wiggle inside shoes just as well, to properly *feel* the ground beneath you.

Imagine the soil beneath you. Yes it's there, beneath all the foundations. Just work through the concrete, wood, whatever – into the earth. There may well be tree roots, insects and small creatures, brick and bone. Just feel it.

Then draw some of that energy up through your feet, into yourself. Take it gently, but let it fill you. Wiggle your feet, fingers, neck and shoulders. Open your eyes. Experience it. See how the world looks now you're actually aware of your connection to it. Remember to breathe.

When you're ready, let that energy flow down again, through your body and out into the earth beneath your feet. Feel yourself still planted, secure and solid. Breathe. Shake your head. Let the excess go.

If you feel wobbly or 'spaced out' at any stage, don't panic – you've just taken on some of the energy from a planet. If you're not used to it, the sensations will confuse you, but this won't always happen. Simply crouch or kneel down, so both your feet (toes are fine) and hands (fingertips) are touching the ground. Let some of the energy discharge down. If it persists, sit or lie down and let it flow from all of you.

For the scientific explanation of what you just did, feel free to investigate books on physics (I find quantum does it best). The idea that all energy is connected is basic, but you are simply working with that connection, sharing energy in the same manner as you share breath with those around you – people, trees, plants, animals, birds… all the same molecules.

When you hold that energy, you can use it for whatever you wish. You can move around – your feet will always be connected to the floor, after all; you're both a conduit and a battery. Ritual, magic, sticking balloons to walls – your choice. But the need for grounding will become apparent from the first time you forget and feel the consequences. It *is* necessary. Don't ever take it for granted.

And, spiritually, I find it's also nice, from time to time, to say 'Thank You'.

The best recent source I've found on energy work, if you want to learn more, is from the late, lamented Isaac Bonewits, in his book 'Real Energy'. Or feel free to reach out and contact me.

What Next?

After I wrote on grounding, the gentleman who inspired the original idea kindly arrived to provide more on the same theme. It's lovely being questioned by folk who genuinely want to know answers (rather than just being polite), but also quite difficult to be approached as some sort of 'Holder of Knowledge'. I find myself replying carefully, allowing understanding, but also because as I hear myself speaking often quite amorphous ideas, I find myself thinking, 'but do I really believe that?'.

A little knowledge can be a dangerous thing indeed. Having picked up some random Paganism 101 books and listened to others of various paths talk, the questions generally ask for clarification on what is 'right', some ultimate truth and correct way of doing things. There does seem to be so much out there now in the way of 'How to Practise (insert path name here)' that I can understand newcomers being overwhelmed. But there is also a certain expectation that there *is* a 'right' path and, if they search hard enough, it will be revealed.

I thought this too, initially. It's the way that we're encouraged to think, from the basic principles taught to us in school. There's a right way to do things, and a wrong way – simple as that, no grey areas. Experienced adults think this too, never having challenged what they have learned, and never seen any reason to.

However, as pagans and responsible, intelligent human beings, I believe we have to constantly challenge and question, in order to find the answers we seek – and, even then, I would be amazed if they are conclusive and final. Answers lead to more questions, after all, and curiosity is inescapable and more *fun*. How boring would life be if we found those 'ultimate answers?' There will always be an 'I don't know', with motivation to look deeper.

But current teaching is only recently starting to recognise the subjective as valid. Previously, the established scientific method (the 'religion' of the 20th century, some would say) has indicated the existence of an empirical, ultimate reality, there for the finding if only we look hard enough. Yet we are taught to take in the information that comes our way, but not necessarily to seek further. There are experts and teachers, whom we cannot question – unless we find a flaw in their thinking, in which case all their work should be disregarded as potentially invalid.

We are all human. We are all fallible. We are all constantly learning. We all have the right to ask questions as we constantly (re)discover how to live our lives day-to-day. Decisions are required and these need information. We cannot know everything, but what resources do we trust to provide data? And how then do we make those decisions?

Here's one. What made you choose paganism (of whichever path) in the first place? How did you research it – books, TV, the internet, other people? At what point did that become not enough, when you finally overcame basic assumptions on learning and went outside to see what was there? Do you still perform ritual outside in all weathers, or do you rush back in to the safe and dry places? Are you at the Questioning stage, or the Accepting stage, comfortable in your knowledge and ability… or not?

So, anyway. Previously it was 'why do we ground?' Now the floodgates are open. Why do we do *any* of the things that modern pagans take for granted?

As more folk have discovered the various paths open to them within paganism, there has been more questioning. I remember finding arguments online and in magazines, questioning the Wiccan Threefold Law, the right to self-initiate, how valid eclectic Pagans were as practitioners (i.e. those who pick and choose their path, usually without a teacher). Some older folk denied the validity of modern Witches unless they could trace their lineage back through various qualified teachers and covens, with proof in their Book of Shadows and the regularity of their rites.

However, as others realised that most modern practices stemmed from Gerald Gardner or Aleister Crowley (or variations thereon), there became more freedom to update a fairly traditional understanding to a more practical way of life-based faith. As a Druid, my practice changes based on such varied factors as how the place I am working feels at the time (location, weather, history, etc.). I have called to the four directions/elements/ quarters based on what is in front of me, rather than how I 'should' do so. I allow my practice to change as I do – as I've said, nothing natural remains static.

This is not with entirely anarchic intention, by the way. I'm not taking down the foundations of modern Paganism just for the sake of it, but because I cannot now stand up honestly and declaim some of the (frankly quite bad) poetry contained in some of the books.

You only have to look at how magic is performed in movies and on television to see how *not* to do things. Apparently magic is reading a poem from a piece of paper, with all the engagement, passion and feeling of a child who has learned something they don't understand by rote. Unfortunately, I have seen this in reality: ritual proclamations read from a laminated card exactly as the teachers at school recited the Lord's Prayer in Assembly – a chore to be worked through because they should.

I can't do this. I can hear my Gods and the universe laughing at me, and I simply can't take it seriously. I cannot express something so fundamentally soulful and dependent on inspiration using fully intellectual methods.

So don't. Say sorry and start again, doing it *better* this time – from your *own* heart and mind. If you don't understand it fully, don't do it. Go away and explore it, *then* try again. I guarantee better results.

The response to rituals I have performed in this way, when

public, has been entirely positive. The most common word is 'powerful'. I believe this is because I keep things relevant, to factors such as location and also who is participating. High Magic (with protractor and compass to have a *perfect* circle, of course) would be pointless when in a park with a circle made entirely of regular folk. I explain and guide as I go along; everyone present is thus comfortable and involved, as their energy focuses on my actions and words, and their understanding grows.

I am no guru. Nor were my teachers, although I respect and honour them hugely. We are all ourselves, practising in our own ways – but as is evident here, I am happy to share this with those who are interested. They question, I answer... where I can. And then we explore together.

Coming?

I'm tired, physically and emotionally. It's been a long weekend. In a field surrounded by woodland with a lake nearby, camping with friends at a re-enactment event, we were supposed to be relaxing. Instead, we were charging about, exploring, catching up with other good folk from around the country that we only see once or twice a year... and engaging in mock battles. I'm only a little bruised, but (as quite a few have commented already) none of us is getting any younger. Next year, everyone promises, will be the year I get fit enough to survive the weekend without getting so bloody knackered. Of course.

One group has pitched their tents next to a beautiful stand of oak trees. I've been nodding greeting every morning to these venerable keepers of the land, who've seen so much – and now this particular brand of human madness. The sound of the wind rustling the leaves calms me, bringing a smile to my face as I listen. A blackbird sings, high in the branches. The coolness of the grass beneath is welcome after a few days of sun-cream application, keeping a supply of water close by at all times to prevent dehydration, and the constant quest for shade while remaining in kit.

I move closer.

'*May I?*'

The response is a sense of curiosity, but polite welcome.

I step up to the trunk, placing one hand on the bark. So much going on here, so much life. One tree among many, one individual supporting and being supported by a multitude of others

As if dreaming, I rest my back against the sturdy oak, closing my eyes as I listen. The wind ruffles my hair as it does the canopy above. My bare feet sink into the ground, deliciously moist, rooting down through my toes.

I hear something and look round.

Some friends are standing nearby, staring. I'm suddenly brought back to myself, aware of what I'm doing. But then I shrug inwardly. Do I care?

"What's up?"

One swallows, finding his voice. "You look... wow. You just look so totally in your element." He smiles. "You look amazing." The other nods vigorously.

My own smile grows wider and I close my eyes again, leaning back as I resume my conversation.

The Need for Protection

To move on a little from grounding to more practical energy work, here's another Pagan Basic: Shielding. Why, How, and What From?

You wouldn't go out in the snow (or sun, or rain) without the appropriate clothing to protect you. Nor tap into a live current, or handle a blazing fire. So why should working with any other sort of energy be different?

I've found a lot of practising Pagans tend to be rather blasé about shielding. It's like stretching before a run – those who know, do. Those who don't... hurt afterwards (and accomplish less).

Why do we assume 'oh, it'll be all right', and then skip it to get to the 'good' bits? Because, quite honestly, that assumption stems from the vague idea that what you're doing *isn't actually that important*. A version of 'it's not really real, so it doesn't matter'.

If that's your point of view, stop with this path. It's not for you. It requires someone who's willing to put in the work at *every* stage, from the foundation upwards.

You're here, so I'm presuming you've some interest in working with energy. Actually, believe it or not, whether consciously in ritual or unconsciously in your daily life... *you already have*. From the nastiness of a crowded shopping centre in the January sales, to the peace of a hilltop at sunset, you will have experienced the feeling of different energies impacting on your own. It's just a matter of working in relationship to that.

This is a key skill within Druidry. If you follow this road, you will find yourself actively noticing those energies daily as you learn more of your connection to the world around. This isn't just for formal ritual.

One of the first things that Paganism 101 teaches us is how to Cast a Circle. Why? Circles are cast to protect, from within and without, both individual or group. But (contrary to what some Ceremonial Magicians will tell you) your own personal circle can be *any* shape. It's yours, after all. It's a matter of focusing on your own energy to affect that around – in other words, magic. Or quantum physics, depending on your point of view.

It's not necessarily all about the correctly coloured candles in the correct places at the correct times, either. It's about you, now, this moment, being able to look after yourself. A little like Pagan Self-Defence. Practise, and after a while, it becomes instinctive.

I've found a variety of ways of creating personal shields. From the slightly ritualised, using ancient mythological symbolism, to a quick visualisation from popular culture, I've worked with ideas suggested to me, translated into a way that works *for me*. When I first started out, I was protecting myself from something both very physical and also intangibly threatening – so I envisaged myself armed with sword and shield. At other times, I surround myself with a net of beautifully crocheted thread, that catches those energies that may harm.

But even now, I can forget... and soon feel the overwhelming awareness of the world taking hold and attempting to drag me under. This isn't necessarily negative or 'evil' – it's just the sheer amount of energy that everything in the world gives off, again consciously or unconsciously.

Consider that crowded shopping centre. The screaming child, the harassed mother, the worried unemployed person, the pain of the old lady in the wheelchair, the tiredness of the staff; multiplied by the number of people. Every curse is a physical blow, every internal sob felt in your own chest. There's no natural light, the very air is recycled, the ground under your feet is concrete above a car park. Your roots can't stretch that far, the natural world seems so far away...

It's not about the formal fighting of mystical demons. It's about using your own focus to protect yourself daily, when such onslaughts occur. They're not necessarily directed at you (although they certainly can be), but you still need to respond.

Yes, it's difficult. This is one of those tasks that is constant practise, every time, because every time, it's a subtly different situation. You still have to deal with it.

One of the quickest ways to protect yourself is to find a quiet place as best you can (a handy bench, a corner booth in a coffee shop, or even the stall of a public lavatory). Centre yourself. Root down, ground if you can. If you're in plain sight, don't worry – everyone else will pass by, thinking you're just having a rest. Close your eyes a little if it helps and is safe to do so.

Imagine a circle around you, coming from within to surround you. Visualise it however you prefer – a bubble, a web, a ball of light, even a circle of thorns. Feel the space inside as your own, protected from the outside hubbub. Breathe. Use a talisman if you find it helps: a necklace pendant, telephone charm or tiny medicine pouch.

You aren't disconnecting from the world. You're standing in your own energy, within it. Know your intention, what you mean that 'safe' energy to be, what its purpose is. Let the protective layer settle around you. Then stand up and go about your business. Finish your tasks and when you're in a place of safety, let yourself breathe out… and the shields can relax. Ground once again, remember your connection. Then – and this is most important – find some solid food.

It's important not to cut yourself off completely. Investing too much energy into those protections for too long can go too far, blocking out the world, so that you're detached and unable to understand or truly see what's going on around you. You're still part of the life on this planet – total disconnection is harmful in itself (worse, in its way, than returning to the 'sleep of ignorance' that most people are content to stay trapped within).

Working with your own energy (as well as that around you) is part of your pagan practice. That's another topic in itself, but the key word here really is 'practise'. Learn your own power and stand in it. If you lose that connection, work to regain it. Exercise, gain strength in your energy.

It's a constant task. But, if we are to live in conscious relationship to the world around, we need to be able to recognise and ride the tides – and know how to help others when they start to sink.

Priorities

Total Stranger: "So what are *you* here for then?"
Me: "Oh, I'm a Druid, here to talk about the Solstice."
Total Stranger: "A *Druid? Seriously? ...* Oh WOW... so, do you, like, dance around trees naked and stuff?"

Me, at the BBC, about to be interviewed on local radio, chatting in the waiting area with a professional journalist. I'd been up since 2am, so he was lucky I just went along with it – although in my defence, I was too tired to do otherwise, and very aware of having my own 'Professional' hat on. But I had my staff with me, and he wanted to talk (another reason that Druids carry them, I'm sure).

I've spoken about labelling, and it will no doubt come up again, particularly with associations such as this that people carry with them. But this illustrates, to me, exactly *why* I was there and talking in public – and why I'm here, writing about it.

We are surrounded by so much information nowadays, we can only take so much in, forcing us to pick and choose what's of interest. Hence the need to pigeon-hole, just for brevity of under-standing if nothing else – I don't expect the average semi-awake BBC Breakfast Show listener to stop what they're doing and listen to me for the three minutes I was on air.

But if even one goes away wondering... and then looks a little more deeply later... they've gone beyond the basic 'hippies in white robes at Stonehenge' that was the germ of why I was there in the first place. So the stereotype has served a purpose, as a springboard for more information to be disseminated and mental pictures to be tweaked.

I am now doing what I do because there are people who would like me to do so. If they didn't, I'd be doing it privately for myself, as I used to do (and still do).

In the meantime, however, daily life has to go on for me, as anyone else. I've had amazement expressed that I have a mortgage, car, bills etc, but that's part of the world today, especially when your 'job' as Druid Priest is not nationally recognised enough to command a salary. It's overwhelming sometimes, too. I claim no Enlightenment, nor personal bliss, and I would be fairly suspicious of any who do.

As awareness grows of the tides we flow in every day of our lives, it's not just information that is too much to take in. Once you have opened up to living, truly *living*, rather than coasting along half-aware between work, family and bed, it's impossible to go back to sleep again. Interest in what's around, curiosity, *awakeness*... and then the 'reality' of apparently normal living crashing in, like an unwelcome force of nature that you can't avoid.

When you're unable to juggle everything that you're *supposed* to do with everything that you know you *should* be doing (and not because you've been told to, but because it's intrinsically more important to your heart and soul), the darkness beckons. Between Magic and Muggledom lies madness – otherwise known as Not Being Able to Tell the Difference.

But you may misunderstand me here. As I've said, magic is unavoidable in life (unless you really try hard), and can be found in the dullest grey office, on the most crowded commuter train, or in the loudest football pitch. Most of all in those places. Spirituality does not require nakedness or a full moon.

My concern is with priorities. Yours and other people's – that's the difference to discern.

"I'd love to do more, you know, magic-y things, but it's just so hard to fit it all in, I never seem to have the time."

I sigh inwardly. How often have I heard that? Childhood religious education teaches that faith is something you do on set days, special occasions, that God will only hear you if you ask in the correct manner, or through the correct intermediary.

The house is old but warm, the kitchen filled with the delicious scents of cooking dinner. Two dogs run around our feet, happily sniffing at the newcomers and the prospect of food. The door bangs as another family member stomps in, banging muddy feet against the step and calling a hello.

She stands in front of me, worried but trying to smile, to be pleasant. A Domestic Goddess. And so she is. Absolutely beautiful, gloriously windswept after a long walk through the woods, juggling family and guests with equal skill, pouring love and energy into everything she touches.

But right now, feeling inadequate because she's 'not good enough' somehow.

"What about dinner?" I ask. The fabulous meal, prepared that day by hand, while performing so many other tasks. An exercise in sheer creative accomplishment. Bubbling pots filled with mystery, to nourish us all.

"Oh, that's nothing. Just food, you know."

I smile. "But you made it. We enjoyed it. It'll keep us going for the rest of the day. And you brought us all together here, like this. That's pretty magic, isn't it?"

Realisation. Her face glows with pride as she finally realises. "A Kitchen Witch, eh?"

Yes. Yes, she is.

My Druidry is not something I put on at weekends. It's something I live. This means that I have certain ethics, a particular way of viewing the larger cosmiverse. That's fine, many people do, and the country I live in allows it to be expressed. I am lucky.

It's when others tell you that you can't that it becomes a problem. That you shouldn't. That you're pigeon-holed – as a Satanist at worst, or a robed nutter at best. I understand the jokes and cat-calls aren't badly meant (usually), but stem from simple ignorance. As transvestite comedian Eddie Izzard said, when he walks down the street, the sight of 'a man in a dress!' equals no frame of reference, momentary panic, then desperate humour.

To which I then respond, laugh, and (hopefully) a conversation ensues.

It's the common ground, the relationship at the heart of us all, that means we should be supporting each other on our own journeys. I'm not out there evangelising – I'm out there being myself. It's up to you how you take that. I can be cynical too, of course, but sometimes I hear myself and stop. The joke isn't funny, even to my own ears. It's not adding anything, it's taking something down. Stop.

The fear, the confusion, the anger – we all feel it, over many different things. If you're sensitive to the energies around, it's a constant whirlpool. All we can do is try to travel with it, helping others along with their flow. We cannot remain static; why do we aspire to? Would that really be any safer?

Yes, I'm afraid a good deal of the time. I don't always know what's ahead, especially when dealing with complete strangers and new situations. But I do my best, stepping forward even a tiny amount at a time, just in case there's a cliff. And if there is... well, I either find my wings or have good friends nearby who can catch me.

So what are your priorities? What are you really *doing?*
And why? Why not?

Stories

So what's your story?

Modern blogging, essentially public journaling, seems to be the twenty-first century equivalent of sitting down with others to tell a tale, to give a little insight into one person's thoughts. We're all curious about others, after all, if only in relation to ourselves – what's normal, what's not. A little glimpse into another's life.

But how often do we allow others time to really tell their tales – and when they do, do we listen?

Buddhists call it 'living mindfully' – really *paying attention* to what is going on around you. From your step on the ground to the breath in your lungs, before you even get to the external world, that multitude of things to be explored. More than a lifetime's work, certainly.

It's not easy. But how often do we even listen to what those we care about are saying? Or do we half-listen... and then misunderstand from that half of the tale?

There have been times when I've not been able to deal with people as much as I'd like – there's simply too much going on in my own head that needs to be dealt with. I've been utterly unable to put on the mask that allows me to go out into the world, smile and do what I'm required to do in my day job. I could not function in the everyday world; it just made no sense to me. But, as I've said before, that is the world in which we live. So what to do?

Having time to really sit and think was one thing (and not initially a good idea, as it is possible to think too much in the wrong direction, especially when ill). But if I was to overcome the blocks inside – if I really *wanted* to – the time had to be recognised as a valuable commodity, taking the opportunity to work through the darkness. Otherwise I would simply be stuck, stagnant and unmoving... and missing *everything*.

This was when I noticed that I had started paying *full* attention to the stories going on around. I devoured movies, DVD box sets, documentaries, novels, travelogues. After each, I would sit and ponder, entirely engaged by the story beyond the basic, the nuances on screen and in text. The currents that make up life, in fact and fiction.

It struck me forcibly that each story was usually set down as absolute truth by its creator. In that contained story-universe, the storyteller was the omnipotent God – so what was s/he choosing to tell us? And if there was trickery or misdirection, why so?

Being so engaged, I found it difficult to follow the trivial, the over-edited reality shows, or even the news – the stories were too brief, too biased, too incomplete. I wanted a truer picture, more points of view. But this is sometimes all we get.

As I came out of myself, this view started to expand. Really paying attention to people again – tentatively fascinated, rather than scared. Meeting new people, letting them talk, laughing with them, seeing their need to be understood as much as I did. And leaving the mask intentionally at home, as I learned to do years ago… and which then, in the interest of self-preservation, had forgotten as I hid behind it again.

I dared to speak my truth to people – and they listened, as I listened to them. More truth followed, as they realised that I was open to them without mockery or sarcasm. The fear of being rejected by the 'normal' wasn't a factor if the common level of humanity was found. This truly is a wonderful thing and, if lucky, great friendships come of it.

Some people don't want to know, of course. That's fine – I encountered that all the time in the City. The masks are too set, the armour to firmly on, with no real wish to look curiously out from behind the security of fear/control. I've been there, and sometimes it's necessary. Not every story is worth listening to, or telling, especially when it's false… and the teller doesn't want you to see what's behind their tale (even if they don't realise the falsity of their words – just look at the motive behind commercials).

But I made my promise. Failing to tell my truth dishonours me and mine. While there are many things that I want to hide from in the world, I can take responsibility; walk away and return (if necessary) later.

I walk on, with honour and bravery, trying to do my best. Even if I fall, the bump and time to sit allows perspective... and the strength to stand up again.

My thanks to all those who value my words enough to listen.

Fear of Listening

I've been asked what is the point of 'being a Druid' in the world today. Well, thinking about what purpose the Druids used to serve in ancient society, that's a good starting point. Briefly, they were the storytellers and seers, but also the lawyers, judges, healers and so forth. A small number of people doing many important jobs. The link between spiritual, social and political life was not so much tacit as unavoidable, intrinsic to the way of life.

Despite the time lapse, how much we've moved on technologically, basic human needs have not changed that much. We cannot take on everything ourselves, nor should we try. There have to be those who can deal with certain situations, who we can call on when needed, from doctors to solicitors.

So how do I 'Druid' every day? That is, aside from the times when I'm professionally 'hired' to perform ritual, or otherwise 'robe up' and grab my staff before heading out. As I've said, spirituality and faith isn't something that you can put on for a special day, then leave aside when going to the supermarket. It's a *Way Of Life*.

When I worked for the Ambulance Service, I wasn't a medic. Most of my working life, I've either been a creative type, or something administrative – I can organise. But even so, when you're standing in public with a uniform on, people will ask questions. As with the robe-uniform, health is a topic that people feel is important and want to talk about, naturally enough, with someone who can advise. So I do my best to advise well, within the limits of my knowledge and training.

However, I then became a member of a Multifaith Board within my local NHS Trust, advising in a pagan capacity, together with a fair few other clever and good-hearted individuals. It was wonderful, as we all did our best to determine the extent to which we could provide support and training to both busy NHS staff and suffering patients. Times of stress are also common to all, especially when in a crisis of health, and faith is something that people turn to, even if they have little experience. Those specifically on call to be sympathetic ears can do a great deal to help heal patients and provide a vital service that harassed and exhausted doctors do not have time for.

Unfortunately, the nervousness that becomes apparent when discussing such issues is immensely saddening. People are afraid to talk about their faith for fear of offending – overworked hospital staff are nervous of asking for help (let alone faith-related help); patients who would like to discuss their terminal illness, for example, are given attention, but not with religious aspects as a priority. While political correctness could have done some good in allowing for Equality policies to become the norm – i.e. respect for all, regardless of orientation or inclination – it seems to have wiped the slate clean somehow, reducing public facilities (including hospitals) to entirely secular environments.

Despite the fact that when you're at a certain level of illness, physical or mental, you need all the help you can get. This doesn't just mean drugs. Most of the time, patients are left alone in rooms or on wards, with no company and no button to press just for someone to talk to. Although this can be requested, as a basic human right, few are informed of that fact.

The secular nature of the world we live in today puts discussing your personal beliefs on a par with discussing a favourite fantasy novel. You're discussing a make-believe world, with superhero deities who talk to you (see Richard Dawkins and his compatriots for more examples!). The fact that you may be simply asking for a vegetarian meal or access to fresh air or a window so that you can see the sky is not important (and is often disregarded). The familiar daily aspects of living your faith are just as important as the formal ritual, but must be requested in an acceptable manner – a difficult thing when in an unfamiliar place, surrounded by strangers. Simple human understanding, at basic level, should be natural.

Most of the patients I saw were afraid. Their bodies or minds were betraying them, going out of control, and they weren't always confident in the care they were receiving. Too many patients, not enough appointments, getting forgotten or not told the full story... healthcare workers do their best professionally, but it's difficult.

While occasionally asked for advice in my capacity as Priest (by staff and 'service users'), I try my best *every day* when faced with suffering. I listen. I talk. When a nurse wheeled up an old lady in a chair, I talked to the lady – who was often shocked by this, as she had previously been ignored, talked around, or spoken to like a child. Often the nurse didn't even know her name. Just showing a little knowledge about their treatment, asking how it's coming along, showing that I care, is enough to bring a fantastic smile. Healthcare Professional, for soul as well as body.

I try to understand.

And why not? As I said, if wearing a uniform (Druid, health services, or anything else), I am approached nervously to be asked a difficult question. Often the questioner is embarrassed and I have to ask them to elaborate, to tell their story. But sometimes just showing that I'm listening is enough. I will advise how best to move forward, but knowing there's a friendly person – where I am, what my name is – means people return, or call me specifically, because they know and trust me. Stress is reduced, problems eased a little.

Even if, unknown to them, I have to take a moment out afterwards because their problems are so momentous, they overwhelm me. Even harder is when treatment fails, and a natural next stage is reached. I have worked with many terminally-ill folk, and have sometimes been the last to listen to them *as a person*. A small candle is lit for a patient. A prayer is said.

Their names are remembered.

My bill-paying work and my Real Work combine in my life. Does this count as Practical Druiding in the Real World? Or just being a caring human being?

Either way, I wish that more people would do it.

Public Ritual

During Spring and Summer, I seem to be most in demand for what I generally term 'Proper Work' – i.e. Professional Druiding. Festivals aside, this is the time when the weather is generally drier, people are shaking off the winter coats, and public rituals are being requested. Since I've taken the decision to put my name out in The World, I do try my best to answer the calls whenever they come, time and distance permitting.

Handfasting ceremonies are becoming increasingly popular, it seems, as couples look to express their love for each other in a lasting and meaningful manner, but without the accoutrements of a faith that is not their own. The connection with nature is commonly felt and, despite the (current) requirement of a legal witness, standing in the wild with those dear to you is a very powerful ritual – and a beautiful memory to keep.

As with any public rite, handfastings always require a good deal of work, but if a couple are happy to entrust me with the responsibility and honour of conducting their own unique day, I sincerely promise to do my utmost to help – and I do.

The duty of a priest is not simply to turn up on the day, dress smartly and say a few words (although I have met a few who seem to think this). From the initial ceremony template through to guarding the handfasting cords the night before, I have been there 24/7 as needed for quite a few people now, and each one has truly been a privilege.

While each day is itself absolutely unique to the couple, there are always a few things that remain memorable. My partner and I keep an informal tally of the new and original catcalls we receive from the general public, usually resulting in us doubled over in laughter (to the confusion of all present): from Harry Potter to Lord of the Rings, we've heard a few. Do we stand out, there in public with robes, cloaks and staff in hand? And what exactly is the correct response to 'wingardium leviosa'?

Rather than being offended, it always makes me smile. The guests gather as far from us as possible, gradually edging forward to ask nervous questions, and often having trouble finding the words. "So… do you do this often? What exactly are you? Do you live in a commune somewhere?"

They're visibly nervous, usually at their first pagan ceremony, but happy to attend out of curiosity and care for those at the centre, the two people joining hands and hearts in a clearly meaningful rite that surprises more than it shocks. When the questions come, I try to answer as clearly as possible, without being too 'cosmic', taking their questions seriously, but in the spirit in which they are asked. On discovering that I have a car, a job and a mortgage, they visibly relax… and the true conversation can begin. Their curiosity can be answered as they listen to what I have to say, relating to me just a bit more as a 'real' person, rather than just a strange woman in robes.

The understanding – and the *wish* to understand – is one of my strongest reasons for continuing to do this. I don't evangelise, but I do try to clarify my truth when asked. As with any conversation, if one side is not willing to listen, then I am not willing to elaborate – but this is certainly the minority rather than the norm.

I'm very glad to say that there's more in common between General Public and Priest than I'd ever have anticipated. Word is clearly getting around – the calls for public ritual keep coming.

And nobody's set fire to me yet.

A wedding at a large public stately home. Lovely. We'd visited beforehand with the couple, discussing the best location, number of guests, practicality of approach, the form of the rite, what to do if it rained. All set.

On the day, we arrive early, as always, to set up and prepare before the guests arrive. Moving quietly through the reception area, a member of staff smiles and points us in the right direction. Pretty clear what we're there for.

As we step out into the beautiful, sunny gardens, I'm almost blinded – by camera flashes. Several dozen guests are already waiting, chatting and nibbling at buffet food, wine in hand. And there I am, robed and cloaked, with drum-bag slung over my back, and staff in hand.

There are plenty of smiles and a good deal of murmuring, but nobody dares to come close. The groom rushes up, clearly nervous but happy, and ushers us through to the small grove that we found for the ritual. Where we discover some occupants.

I quietly walk up to the staring teenagers, sitting on the grass with their cans and bottles surreptitiously wrapped in paper bags. It's a public place, they have every right to be there. I just have to hope for the best.

"Hi – we'll be performing a pagan wedding here in a little while. Would you like to stay and watch?"

They're frozen. I wonder how I appear to them. But then they nod. I continue to smile, thank them, and walk away to prepare the space.

The rite is perfect. The couple make their vows, well supported by friends and family. I look up as the circle is closed, and realise that we're surrounded by people – not only invited guests, but many strangers who passed by and stopped to watch, as well as the entire staff of the house and the band who will be playing at the reception. I brace myself for the inevitable Q&A period that will ensue after the photographs.

As we pack up the bread and mead, I see one of the teenagers coming towards me. Clearly petrified, he bobs up and down, as I would imagine a nervous messenger with bad news would before a tyrant lord. I smile encouragingly, if a little nervous myself. What can he possibly want?

He takes a deep breath and lets his words out in a frantic rush.

'"I just wanted to say thank you – my girlfriend's into Wicca, and I... well, I didn't really know much about it, but I really enjoyed that, it was amazing, thank you so much."'

His friends are staring at him from a safe distance, and I realise the sheer guts that it has taken him to come and speak to me. I thank him, slightly overwhelmed. He'll never know how much he has honoured me with those few simple words.

I make my offerings of thanks as the wind sings gently through the trees, and take my own deep breath, before moving back towards the party.

From the Darkness...

In every story, there is a challenge to be overcome – that's part of life, this Hero's Journey that we all walk every day. But how often is that challenge the overcoming of personal darkness? Not glamorous, but deep, painful and with no guarantee of a light at the end.

Life is not an either/or of light and dark. I'm sometimes confused by pagans whose purpose in their work seems to be to 'bring light to the world'. The principle is noble, but the reality would be fearsome if followed through to its natural conclusion. Nature's balance is not a straightforward binary, nor does it follow humanity's ethical priorities.

We need the darkness as much as the light. One cannot exist without the other, but more often it is true to say that both exist in close relationship. Too much of either and we are simply left blind.

The balance is a fine one, and few of us are unaware of it. Cerridwen's cauldron inspired... and also poisoned. Merlin held the life of the land, before going mad in the forest.

These are not stages we should close our eyes too. We cannot hide from the dark (what's inside our own eyelids, after all?), but it is part of the journey to see the difficulties that may be encountered as we brace ourselves to walk into those dark and unknown woods.

The possible link between creativity and manic-depression is now starting to be investigated in more depth, by academics (and sufferers) such as Kay Redfield Jamison. Children are being made aware of both the joys and depths to be experienced in life, in artists such as Vincent Van Gogh, in 'Doctor Who', or the manic tattooed mother in the work of Jacqueline Wilson.

Part of the journey of the Druid is to step into the dark woods, both externally and within ourselves. The Bard is the ultimate creative, channelling inspiration to make something powerful from his passion. The Ovate takes this further, journeying intentionally into the darkness to find healing and knowledge until his eyes turn black with what he sees (according to the Welsh tales).

And it hurts. I've received treatment for depression, due to various external hurtful events in my life all arriving at once, but while not manic, I've experienced those deepest of lows, as so many of us have. I now realise that I can't just 'keep calm and carry on' – nobody can. I sometimes have to take myself away in order to reconnect, to pull myself back out again from that pit of confusion, so that I can function in the everyday world.

I've seen countless articles on how more people are going through such times, with general reflection on how it is the fault of the world and the society that we live in. Perhaps. But saying this is part of the human condition is untrue – non-human animals clearly feel both sadness and joy. Emotions exist for a reason, whether they be pleasant or not. It is up to us how we explore them and use them to move forward.

Spiritually, I try to use the knowledge and experience of my own darkness to help others as best I can. Sometimes, even the knowledge that there are other people who have been through what you are yourself suffering is enough; sometimes you need someone to be there with a cup of tea, holding a candle to aim towards, or a metaphorical rope to get you out of the hole. Sometimes you need a partner to sit down there with you, just being there. Your own space is important, but it can be your own worst enemy – and you're not always the best judge when vision's clouded by the darkness.

It's never easy to understand, but it's part of life. When the connection to life is lost, then that candle is in danger of flickering out – the depressive suffers the ultimate 'side-effect' of their illness, as did Van Gogh and so many others. It is up to us to remember that the connection is always there.

Step outside. Reach for a trusted hand. Make and enjoy a cup of tea. But see the value in that connection and channel it as best you can. As I am here, right now.

We walk onwards.

Dark Mythology

Let's talk about Gods.

A friend of mine was once told that apparently, according to some other pagans she'd spoken to, it wasn't appropriate for her to have the Morrigan as a patron deity, as 'she's too dark'. She should pick someone who was better, nicer. More Good. Nothing shocking.

Now leaving aside the whole 'picking deity' thing, I'd like to talk about the so-called 'dark' gods.

(And I'm assuming that if you're here, you have some knowledge of mythology, gods in general as archetypes, and how they are used/ envisioned in paganism. We're not going to talk about 'what is a god', that's for another time. Still here? Lovely.)

Hades. Efnisyen. Loki. Hekate. The Morrigan. Ereshkigal.

Say any of these at a pagan gathering, and I've found there's always someone who'll look at you as if you just said 'Satan', in the Dennis Wheatley sense. For some reason, Loki in particular appears to be anti-flavour of the month at the moment, although I've no idea why.

Darkness exists. Every day, for a good few hours, in fact – it's called night-time, and it isn't actually intrinsically evil, it's just that time when the sun is on the other side of the planet from us right now. It also exists in deep cupboards, under beds and the wardrobes of goths, but I think you get my point. It's there.

Unfortunately, some pagans seem to believe that if we only believe in the concept of 'light', the darkness will be somehow banished. Darkness = evil, light = good, and related gods correspond accordingly.

This actually makes no sense to me at all. It possibly stems from the old fear of the dark, with lack of light to prove that no nasties were hiding where you couldn't see, and from which they could leap out at you (i.e. aforementioned deep cupboards). Lack of control over environment = potential evil. Fair enough, that's animal instinct for you. Survival mechanisms.

But surely it's truer to say that as everything is best in moderation, both dark and light (as energy) can be both good *and* bad? Even as too much darkness is frightening, too much light is blinding.

If this related to Christian mythology, with the darkness before Creation equalling Chaos and nothingness, the Old Testament proves that Jehovah had his moments of both benevolence and vengeance. I know it's apparently impossible for him to be 'bad' by definition, but even looking at him or hearing his voice meant death to the poor human on the receiving end ('We went through five Adams before we figured that one out.'[2]). Even if He is somehow solely, inarguably 'good' in a human, ethical sense, it is clearly not true that all Christians are likewise – as I'm sure those on the receiving end of the many Christian wars would agree. The same holds true for most of the major dogmatic faiths.

Similarly, saying Hekate is patron of witches, with its direct associations with evil and wartiness as per Shakespeare, immediately misrepresents all witches – who aren't. It's a gross generalisation, often for the purpose of simplistic propaganda and ignoring the multi-dimensional reality or relevance of the image.

I'm not trying to be wishy-washy and relativistic – this isn't about how the poor deities mentioned above are nice really, just terribly misunderstood, poor dears. It's more that our understanding of them is severely limited, to the point where we miss the point of the 'dark' gods as necessary to life. Not everything in life is good, and if anyone believes that it is, good luck to them.

While it is a matter of perspective, if you believe that each deity holds certain characteristics at some 'uber'-level, thus making them an ultimate patron of that aspect (i.e. music, wisdom, crocodiles, computers), you are following a fairly ancient viewpoint. The Romans, Greeks etc believed this, so far as we know from those writings remaining, and made offerings accordingly. The gods were indeed 'childlike and capricious'. Jehovah then arrived, embodying *everything*, soon followed by the Great God of Science, both pooh-poohing all that had gone before. We now achieve understanding of the universe as we each think best, according to a combination of societal or personal philosophy... and so here we are as twenty-first century pagans.

However, if you are to believe that deity is more representative of aspects of humanity at this uber-level, it must reflect humanity as it is at *any* given point in time or space. We, now, cannot truly understand the complex beliefs of ancient societies as they were lived. Nor do we really need to, except possibly at an intellectual level of (dis)provable data. Humanity as a species is fairly constant in its needs and priorities. We are exploring ourselves and our lives, where *we* stand in the universe. Deity helps this. As we are not one-dimensional beings, nor should they be.

In fact, I would argue that most of the more famous pagan deities *aren't*, at all. Let's take Loki again. I've received shocked looks when mentioning him. So, in the interests of exploring and confronting fears, I tried working with him. There, I said it, and I'm not in the least ashamed.

Loki was fated to kill Baldur, and so he did, remaining true to his nature and destiny and being condemned for it. But it is fairly true to say that throughout his career as 'trickster', he was quite often the only Norse god who did act honestly. He was truthful, when truth equalled pain... those truths that nobody wants to hear. Hence the wry smile, because he knows nobody will admit that they understand him. But we all know such a feeling, like it or not. *Schadenfreude.* The basis for a lot of 'harmless' modern comedy.

Efnisyen, from the *Mabinogion* stories. Famously out of control, jealous and angry. Who can honestly say that they have never felt such emotions? But he has the honesty to act on them, which is hard for us to swallow because we want to be seen as 'good' and 'controlled', when what we really want to do is smash things.

Hekate. The Crone, holder of ancient wisdom. We might not know her yet, but we can hope to one day. Except as she is depicted, so we disregard or mock old women who look like witches. Shallow and ignorant, we ignore her deeper truths and the knowledge she holds, because it's not easy to reach, and not pretty when we get there. There is wisdom in her cauldron, but it's life experience that we're not willing to look at. We can't get past the surface, because we don't really want to.

The dark gods reflect a large part of life. We should *not* ignore them, nor our own personal darkness. If we do, we're like the foolish pagans who stood chanting around an overheated and dehydrated person at a Pagan Camp, rather than fetching them water and shade (yes, really). Belief must be relevant and applicable, not carried out ritualistically 'because it should'.

We use the tools we have to live well every day. As pagans, we have slightly different tools to others due to our beliefs and methods of understanding. Deity as archetype assists with this, whether by deeper investigation of mythologies for human truths, or even simply speaking to them directly. Lessons should be learned at a level beneath the surface for greater comprehension. Be curious – *why* did someone act the way they did? This is true for anyone, human or other, but especially in stories that have struck a chord and endured – the method by which the gods travel and teach.

But the ultimate test is when someone close to you dies.
This will happen to all of us.
What is our understanding of it?

Generally death is ignored, but this just makes it harder to face when the time comes. Whether by imagining Death as a large black-cloaked skeleton with a scythe or a small goth girl with an umbrella, it helps to have someone to talk to, even if just as a personification to aid the process of grieving and healing. Someone who's an expert, who has been doing what they do for far longer, and has a cosmically greater understanding of its meaning than you. If you're one of those who believe that deity is formed from the beliefs of many, then imagine how much energy is invested in those so familiar to us all.

The crux of the dark deities is that they don't sugar-coat the facts, but tell us what we need to hear. The question is whether we are ready to truly hear it. This by no means makes it 'evil', just a difficult part of life.

So investigate. Talk. Acknowledge the darkness as inevitable, not automatically a monster. And as you will see when standing outside on a freezing winter night… the dark can be beautiful.

Inspiration and Deity

Quite a few years ago, when more concertedly seeking training and information, I posted a question on a forum for Druid discussion. I was curious, so I asked those who might know the answer (as you should):

'Druidry today primarily focuses on the power of inspiration, the Awen that flows through everything. Should we therefore not be seeking that connection all the time, to some degree?'

I was younger; I'd never ask that now, because I know better. While connection is always present while we live in the world, constantly channelling that Awen would probably have exploded my mind and sanity very quickly, should I have ever discovered how. Imagine being 'tuned in' to the universe at all times. Too much for a human mind, except in small doses!

But to put it more correctly as to what I was feeling *then*, I was really asking whether we as Druids should be constantly seeking our muse, our creativity, to fuel our joy of life. We all know how hard it is to get bogged down, and walking our talk was (and is) a real challenge for me. From what I'd found when looking, it seemed that nobody actually did know how to express this (and I certainly didn't intend to wander around robed up and covered in crystals 24/7 in an effort to find out).

The answers I got from the forum weren't terribly inspiring themselves, to my surprise. In the usual manner of the internet, I was scoffed at, my ignorance mocked, a few extremely impractical suggestions thrown in, but very little suggested in the way of realistic steps towards my intended goal.

Which said to me: 'They don't know either.'

Now, looking back, I think this is partly true... but also partly an issue of expression. How do you express inspiration, and the finding of it, the living of it? All of the poets and a good deal of the writers throughout human history have tried. Shakespeare invokes his muse at the start of his plays, the Greeks likewise voiced their plea for inspiration in the voices of their Chorus. Most recently, I laughed aloud at Selma Hayek in the movie 'Dogma'[3], a muse seeking her own inspiration (in the oddest places, true, but ones that I'm sure worked for Kevin Smith).

I then found the following on an audiobook, and rather loved it. Don't be put off by the language – read it over until parts start to jump out:

'Invocation

State your intentions, Muse. I know you're there.
Dead bards who pined for you have said
You're bright as flame, but fickle as the air.
My pen and I, submerged in liquid shade,
Much dark can spread, on days and over reams
But without you, no radiance can shed.
Why rustle in the dark, when fledged with fire?
Crazy the night with flails of light. Reave
Your turbid shroud. Bestow what I require.
But you're not in the dark. I do believe
I swim, like squid, in clouds of my own make,
To you, offensive. To us both, opaque.
What's constituted so, only a pen.
Can penetrate. I have one here. Let's go.'[4]

This from a book written in recent years, whose sheer size is enough to daunt, but once penetrated, is absolutely inspiring. The muse did indeed answer the author's request.

I saw a documentary with Terry Jones (former Python and extremely loveable wit) in which he actually showed his process of 'Summoning the Muse'. It involved sitting at his desk, pen and paper primed... and then spending as long as it took to come up with something useable. Chewing the pen, doodling, fiddling about, hum-te-tum, no that's rubbish... but not leaving that desk.

Not at all magical, but it worked.

I don't spend a lot of time agonising about what I'm going to write. I ponder a little and ideas come, then I start typing and see how the words flow. But then I have unofficially had writer's block for the last ten years or more – I used to write story as if I was possessed. Life then changed, and so did the form of ideas moving from brain to page.

I'm often asked about Gods. "What Gods do you worship?" someone queries nervously. I respect them for actually voicing their curiosity, but I honestly have no idea what they expect my answer to be. The question often seems to be more 'How do you step out of the 'normal' life we all live, what else is there, show me the magic...' or suchlike.

I was asked to sincerely consider this question once. So I did. And in turn, I found it hard to clearly express my conclusion in a manner that could be understood by those who have not gone through similar experiences.

As the poets found, I believe that those deities we are subject to are those forces far larger than ourselves, but which compel our lives. Inspiration is one of these, called on by many. Sometimes by name, as Brigid, Muse, or even Shakespeare or Byron themselves. I absolutely acknowledge those specific facets of spirit, male, female or other, but when I call on my Gods, I invoke those universal forces... in the full knowledge that this will be far more than I can handle (and not always in the form I expect), but if you don't ask, you don't get.

I'm not daft enough to believe that I can control the universe. But I do aspire to work with my relationship as part of it. Universal forces are far more than I can understand – and ultimately, why should they care about me? It's more about relationship, understanding and perception.

'A child may step out into the rain and the shock of connection provokes a wail of discomfort, while another might feel the song of the

rain approaching, and when it comes welcomes it with with a soul
utterly receptive to its music, her own soul dancing with the harmonies
she makes with the soul-song of the rain.'[5]

Druid author Emma Restall Orr, summing things up very well
indeed.

We are part of nature. We can call on those parts that we are
connected to, with our understanding allowing us to work with
them through experience and respect. My issue with the
'accepted' faiths is that you are expected to bow down to a
greater power. I don't understand this, not as an issue of ego, but
because I perceive that any person cowing to such a force will
simply get swept away (usually with mocking laughter). Your
perspective can allow you to understand, but you must approach
those greater powers with honesty of intention – otherwise your
understanding will be false, coloured by the filters of bullshit that
you surround yourself with. Terry Pratchett understands this
very well, as do a surprising number of other modern creative
folk (as above).

In all of my writing, including this book, it is my intention to
create and assist understanding – not necessarily encouraging
my own 'way', but more stimulating curiosity to find your own
path and walk it. This is the reason that I'm standing up and
declaring myself, whether I'm heard or not. I state my belief, and
that's mine – if it encourages even one other person to find their
connection, fantastic. But I'll still be on my path over here if I'm
needed.

Incidentally, I may not always be right, but am more than
happy to enter into discussion and conversation. Change is
inevitable; I'd be the first to say I don't know everything, as my
life goes on and my perception evolves. But this is my perspective
now. Challenge me if you wish, but only if you do so with respect
and honour. Flaming, trolling, raising oneself on the backs of
others – that's the opposite of what I seek.

I've discovered that I cannot live responsibly and honourably and still bow down to the deities dictated by others, whether 'on high' or simply corporate. I am part of the society of this country, yes, and so subject to its laws. I may not agree with them all, but I seek understanding as part of my relationship. Simply whingeing and expecting others to sort matters out will get me nowhere.

I have chosen my way as priest, and I have my voice – here it is. Even if my questioning causes confusion. If you don't see the need to constantly question, you might be better going back to sleep.

So I call on the Awen to help me in this mad quest that is life, to capture some portion of its essence in words – to inspire others to seek it out, by whatever means they find best. May they find joy and fulfilment in their connection.

And doing so every day is what Druidry is for me. A lived faith, of relationship and inspiration.

Pilgrimage

As recommended by Druid musician and songwriter Damh the Bard recently, I'm reading the excellent and thought-provoking 'Earth Pilgrim' by Satish Kumar. The following passage struck me and stayed with me:

> Narrator: To be a pilgrim is to walk the talk. When you're a pilgrim, it's not the physical difficulties you face when you're walking – it's the mental difficulties that arise within you that are so challenging. So... what is the difference between ordinary everyday life, and being on a pilgrimage?
>
> *SK: For me, there is no difference: life itself is a pilgrimage. To be a pilgrim is to be on the move, physically, mentally and metaphorically. Life is a pilgrimage because life is not static. Life has no ultimate objective. Life is to be lived in every moment. The meaning of life is in the living. As a pilgrim, I discover the mystery, the magic, the meaning, the magnificence of life in every step I take, in every sound I hear, in every sight I see.*
>
> *Taken from 'Earth Pilgrim'*[6]

Now, if you check the biography of the author, you will see that he has indeed been an active pilgrim for most of his life, as a Jain monk. Very few of us have the freedom or inclination to do that – and as he says himself, the pilgrimage has become rather an alien concept to the European mind. We modern types prefer tourism, utilising the environment, rather than passing through it as witnesses.

But, as I've said before, we're all walking our own paths, our own stories. That's life, we can't really do anything else. So, while we may benefit from practising Buddhist-style mindfulness, being truly aware of our own pilgrimage as we walk it, our Western minds may find this far too hard a task, if not nigh on impossible. And would not such over-intellectualisation cause its own difficulties? If we're constantly second-guessing our routes in life, a future we cannot possibly see except in anticipatory dreams, does this not cripple us as to which decision to make... thus stalling any movement at all?

Einstein famously said: 'Life is like riding a bicycle. To keep your balance, you must keep moving.' Even those who stay virtually comatose in front of their televisions all day are alive and moving... but not, it is true to say, really *living* to their fullest potential, as they neither learn nor progress.

Perhaps some forms of modern life are more like the hamster-wheel of a static bicycle – risk-free, supported fully, yet going nowhere.

If we take time to pause, take a break and review, we find it is actually easy to see the route our paths have taken so far: the diversions, side roads, branches and U-turns that we have made, either voluntarily or at the behest of another. Thus we are here, now; pilgrims to our own futures. So how do we feel, as we pause to take stock? Does this help us realise we might need to change direction a little, perhaps seek a map or a guide through the places we've been avoiding?

I was introduced to paganism via witchcraft and Gardnerian Wicca, moving through the bookshelves of my local chain bookstore to investigate many other traditions, finally encountering Druidry. Which, as others have said more eloquently than I, sums up better than any other the way I view the world, and how I wish to practise.

I took the plunge (literally), spending time on retreats and sweat-lodges, undertaking intense Druidic training with wonderful but demanding teachers. Inevitably, my life changed as a result of these decisions. Each of the major steps I have taken has resulted in marks (both mental and physical) and promises – which I have kept, through many ups and downs.

Now, I do my best to stand up and walk my talk. To do

otherwise would be a virtual U-turn, and I don't think that's possible any more. Together with those who wish to accompany me, I move forward, on my own life-pilgrimage.

So as others have previously borne witness, I present once again my promise made as a member of the Order of the Yew:

I step upon the earth.
Step. Step. Step.
Hard, soft.

Blood of many gone before, blood of many invisible now. Sleeping plants, busy insects, life beneath me, beside me, above me... inside me.

Blood, never stops moving. My own world, walking the world around. Being present, unable to step away. How is it possible to distance yourself when every breath carries so much? Riding the tides, dancing the fire, singing the wind, feeling the earth.

I make my promise, feeling the fear and weight of my words. I make my promise to live, passionately, fully and completely, ethically and in Truth. I anticipate the stumbles, but pledge to always dance back to my path, through dark and light, easy and hard. To live as the ancestors wish.

To bring my courage, strength, respect and honour to my daily tasks, inspiring those around as best befits. Expanding my truth, to affect the world about me with its fire – creativity, love and laughter. A candle flame in the dark... the hardest and yet easiest to light and hold.

I feel the fire burning in my big black pot. I feed it to nourish me and mine.

Paganism and the Weather

I was once called by a local BBC radio station, entirely out of the blue, and asked if I would like to come on their breakfast show to talk about paganism in relation to the 'weird weather we're having'.

I was slightly flummoxed by this. *What* weird weather? We live in England! The weather is doing what it always does – being unpredictable! But hey-ho, on we go.

I had to pre-record a little five-minute interview beforehand over the telephone, just in case I couldn't make it onto the show live. And the first thing the researcher asked?

"So, can you control the weather?"

I sighed.

Right. Thanks to that little gem, I'm now fully warned that I'm being brought on as The Pagan Fringe Nutter. Except no – I'm not going to live up to that. Sorry.

Those who heard it and reported back were entirely positive, for which I am always grateful. I am always nervous about speaking publicly, but am now aware through experience of How to Act on Radio. No easy sound-bites, remember to smile even though they can't see you (it comes across in your voice), and explain *properly*. Imagine all the everyday folk listening who know nothing about what you're talking about, and wouldn't understand a metaphor if they were burning it at the stake.

So I hear the weather-lady chatting about it beforehand to the producer. She sounds as confused as I am about why they're asking such ridiculous questions ('Will it be a typical October?'). But then she articulates clearly on the air about the reasons for the hot July and relatively mild and rainy August, in the meteorological sense. Lovely.

Now me.

The response when I spoke of this on my blog was largely

humorous, unsurprisingly. Talk of wasting licence fees, how *does* Paganism relate to the weather (causing torrential rain when inconvenient, apparently) etc. But actually, on consideration... it does.

I spoke of the handfasting I'd officiated the previous weekend. Torrential bursts of rain from midday over Nottingham, everyone worried about it ruining the outdoor ceremony. When it came time for the bride and groom to emerge into the beautiful wooded grove, the sun is shining and the sky is blue. I've never had a public rite that was spoiled by weather (yet). This impresses people, and makes me smile.

So does this mean that I 'controlled' the weather? No. It means I looked behind the clouds scudding overhead to see the blue sky coming, and asked the Powers That Be to be timely with it. A little weather knowledge, use of my eyes and a sense of relationship... and all is well.

It's not an issue of 'Control'. In this modern world, where darkness is beaten back by electric lighting and the seasons are seen as an inconvenience by many, we are in fact still subject to earthly phenomena out of our control. Floods happen. Droughts happen. We must prepare for these as best we can, as has humanity throughout history. We cannot build on a flood plain and then complain about rain washing us out. We must factor the unexpected into our plans (reasonable risk, I believe it's called nowadays).

I spoke of how this rankles with our sophisticated twenty-first century mindset. We don't like to think we're at the mercy of larger forces than ourselves. We don't like to see that we're just another species on a very large planet, and that we have to share with others, whose priorities may be different. We don't like to see that what we do affects that relationship (i.e. rainfall as a result of pollution).

We like to think that we're advanced, beyond worrying about seasons and suchlike. Yet the proof is clear: Russia experienced a bad harvest, which affected grain prices for England. We can complain about the price of bread, but we fail to see the cost in life and effort as it moved from the fields to our supermarket shelves.

The community we live in may be widening, but we're still part of it, and this cannot be denied.

As a Pagan and a Druid, I feel this as part of my sense of relationship with the land that holds me, the sea that surrounds this island and the sky above us all. If something is needed, I ask. Call it prayer, what you will, but I have found that if I ask with honest intent and for honourable reason, things tend to happen. This isn't control. This is relationship.

I spoke of the Harvest Festivals, the deep history of farmers working with the land to influence a good crop. The corn dollies, the sacrifices. Schools still celebrating, even if they don't entirely know why. English produce in local branches of national chain stores, from our own trees rather than overseas, with its own unique taste. Appreciating our place in the world, how we affect it and how it affects us. We're foolish to fight this and then wonder why we lose.

I was actually asked to return the following Sunday, to speak more on this topic as part of the radio station's religion programme. Wicker men were mentioned (inevitably). The DJ was openly Christian and fairly nervous. But I spoke of the joy of our relationship with our land, the beauty of creating a person out of windfall to celebrate the season. The fact that while the King used to be sacrificed bodily to the land, the Queen today has virtually sacrificed her life for her people. There will always be parallels, as human nature flows.

I didn't mention the spirits of the land, the air, the rain. That would be going a little too deeply into matters that cannot be explained simply in a five-minute interview. I did what I always do when acting publicly: I try to instigate curiosity, inspire thought, make an audience look deeper.

Weather is inevitably a part of life, be it heat, rain or snow. As is my faith, in all its facets and seasonal aspects. So they are linked. This is what I try to help others understand.

Shortly after this came the Winter Solstice, the shortest day of the year, and the longest night. More or less the whole of Britain was experiencing intense disruption as a result of the most serious snow and ice seen since the big freeze of 1963. Being British, people complained, wondering when the snow will be gone, what could be done about it, and who to blame. Similar to the disruption caused to airline travel by a volcanic ash cloud affecting atmospheric conditions earlier in the year. Who provides compensation for Acts of Nature?

Some were unable to travel overseas for their holidays, or to see family. Some were unable to leave their houses, and had neighbours bring them food. All of us became more restricted to our immediate communities.

Expecting 'business as usual' under such circumstances is unrealistic, if not impossible. The weather really is the ultimate in uncontrollable forces of Nature, reasserting itself to remind us of our place, despite all our clever technology.

So how far removed are we, with our credit cards and Christmas lights, when things cannot be brought to our doors from far away, when our expensive cars cannot take us beyond the driveway – when we have to simply submit to what is actually a normal winter?

Solstice morning. My partner and I bundle up as best we can and set out with an excited puppy, walking to the top of our hill as the first greys of dawn touch the clouds. Icy grass crunches as the light changes to let us see.

As the sky transforms from night to day, the atmosphere itself changes too. It doesn't grow noticeably warmer, but things around us slowly begin to awake. The lights of persistent commuter headlights slowly come into view through the trees. The farmer nearby begins to lead his cows out to their own snowy fields. A flock of ravens wakes up loudly and begins to search for breakfast. Other dogs greet us, taking their owners out for their walks.

The Earth moves, as it does constantly, but somehow more visibly on the Solstice, when you're actively standing, watching, waiting for the sun. So, so slowly this year, the tension palpable. I half wonder if it's going to rise at all, realising how the ancestors must have felt at such a time.

We need the sun to rise. We need the Spring to return. We need this festival of light to remind us that the trees will bloom again, the land will return to lush greenery and we won't always lose feeling in our fingers a minute after we've stepped outside. But we can't force it to conform to our schedule. We can simply have faith.

The beauty of the sky is almost tangible. Sudden oranges glow off the clouds, incredible peaches and cream shadings. A single star glows. The moon stays hidden behind the first lunar eclipse this century. The balance is clear – summer and winter, night and day, sun and moon, oak and holly.

And then there it is. The sun is risen. People at the nearby bus stop are laughing. Gifts are given, blessings sent via immediate electronic message. Marvels old and new, but expressing the same joy.

In the midst of winter, the world still turns. We are part of the cycle, not its masters. And so, we celebrate.

Spirits of Place

Here's something everyone can relate to. Compare places you've been: small towns, big cities, imposing mountains (top and bottom). Different countries. Different times of year.

Every place has its spirit. Whether a clear personification (such as Sulis at Bath or Sabrina along the River Severn) or just a general feeling, we can all call to mind the different energies of places that we have experienced.

And so we do. Aware or not, think of the times you've chosen one destination over another, because one feels right or another makes you just shudder. Putting such a feeling into words is difficult, and certainly not always explainable. Stepping over the threshold into a place of burial brings its own sense of quiet. A particularly powerful sacred site can inspire quiet joy, bubbling in the belly as every step connects you to... something.

If you're particularly in tune with these energy flows, this will not come as news to you. But how often do we respect those spirits of place, acknowledge them and flow with them, rather than trying to fight against them? How often are we responsible for them, evolving them with our own energies as we pass through even briefly?

Working daily in London and taking my earlier steps along the pagan path, I discovered that while most self-professed Pagans live in cities, very few actually seem to *like* it. Given half a chance, they'll hare off to the country to dance barefoot in the woodlands (presumably not pine forests, though – ouch!) or camp out under the stars... until the need for running water and television sends them home again.

Coming from various small villages in the South of England, I could never get over the fact that I've always been the 'country mouse', even after almost a decade in our capital city. I accli-mated for a while – finding my way on the Tube without getting lost, navigating during bomb threats, giving directions to tourists – but now, living in a village in the East Midlands, I look back with a sense of amazement. As I've said before, a good deal of city living seems to be about constantly shielding yourself from the world around, just to survive the chaos of so much going on. Understandable, really... but terrifying also, as each person loses their connection, seeing the world around through a fog of their own making. And still looking for answers to why they're so lost.

But one thing London did teach me was that as I learned to open myself up again, I also found myself becoming more aware of the flows around me, reminding me of playing in the woods as a child. It's natural, after all – you're part of your surroundings, like it or not. *You* contribute to the spirit of that place. It just depends whether the woods are made of trees or buildings... and how you prefer to play.

I've read many accounts of the spirit of London. It is all of those things: Charles Dickens' workhouses and lawyers, Neil Gaiman's street fairies and homeless, Michael Moorcock's industry, Doris Lessing's confusion, Peter Ackroyd's biography. Each theatre and film adaptation captures a tiny facet of the whole. Which is, ultimately, what we are, attempting to understand it. A Canary Wharf businessman tells the tale of London as much as the Waterloo homeless girl with her dog.

A friend of mine put it most succinctly:

The cities were made by those people, for those people. I think it's more about the attitudes that are then held, as folk take their surroundings for granted (i.e. dropping litter, noise pollution, etc). If more people saw that history, scale and beauty, that could only have impact in their realisation. While it IS there for their use, it shouldn't be taken for granted; we're all part of making it what it is.

I've been fortunate enough to meet quite a few others who feel likewise. Discussing city magic, 'pavement fairies' (our term!), I've skipped through the snow, arm in arm with a like-minded laughing lunatic, parting the lawyers on Ludgate Hill and Fleet Street as they watched in amazement (I saw some secret, longing smiles). I've guided frightened tourists through lightning storms, told stories to strangers on buses of the history of the buildings we were passing, struck up conversations with surprised folk on trains about the book they were reading, danced in ecstasy between shop awnings during a cloudburst after a drought.

That certainly isn't 'proper' London behaviour – but such wonderful madness clearly *is* what's needed sometimes. My time in the capital was clearly about to be up. Ready to move on to other places to see what they feel like.

The spirit of place is there if we open ourselves to it. You won't be able to anticipate what will come, not really – it's far bigger than we are, certainly larger than can be comprehended intellectually.

But we're part of it, wherever our feet happen to be standing at that precise moment. It is respectful to acknowledge it, to truly *see* and give greeting, even a nod in passing – because that's what we're doing. Passing through, bringing what we have, and taking a small memory of how that place felt, how it affected us (good or bad). Make friends with it, if it seems like your sort of person.

We're taught as children to give thanks to kind hosts after a party. Thank you, spirits of place, for such a lovely time. I hope to be able to come back again.

Stories Again

I seem to keep coming back to this, but the idea, perception and reality of Story is a constant in my life.

When acting as a 'public Pagan', there are occasional sudden surges of interest from the mainstream world, at solstices and equinoxes, Samhain and Beltane. I've had television cameras in my home, my workplace and generally following me for an entire day, for a clip that lasted two to three minutes, broadcast on October 31st. It was constantly stated that everything we did must be accurate... and then polite requests to move things, dress differently and ultimately be tweaked in my presentation for 'better television'.

And this is what got me thinking. While it's flattering to have interest, especially when positive (as seems to be the case these days) rather than 'look at those weirdos', each time I try to prepare as best I can, with a small and simple tale to summarise myself and my pagan life. The interviewer then asks the strangest things, and an entirely different story is created and broadcast. Which is why I prefer live broadcasts to recorded ones, even if you have to be fully on the ball and prepared for odd surprises (see my previous tale about controlling the weather).

But isn't this ultimately the best we can do? When people ask *any* given question, you can only give a potted slice of life, perspective and opinion, while understanding and interest are maintained. And, even then, while you may say one thing, interpretation is another matter entirely. People may speak of you, or relate events that bear no resemblance to your own recollection. In that sense, your story is entirely out of your own control – even when recorded. How far can you influence other people's preconceptions, through changing their assumed knowledge?

Put simply, it's another reason that I'm writing this now. If it (hopefully) makes you, the Reader, a little more curious, more inspired, it's a way for me to constantly relate, update and advance my own story while influencing yours in a positive way. A true and generous relationship, from both sides.

If folk are interested in my words, great! If further questions are asked, even better. I like to tell stories, always have. They can be taken and understood how they will – I have no control over that, nor would I really want any; just a little more under-standing. I'm only one voice.

But this then brings me to what is 'true'. Without going into the nature of truth as a philosophical concept (go look it up, it's fascinating. And very much *not* set in stone), the main reason behind all of the media attention in 2010 – aside from the timing of Samhain – was the Charity Commission's decision to grant The Druid Network charity status.

The media, other individuals, other groups, had all taken this relatively simple announcement and interpreted it in their own manner. Mostly positive, but by no means all. I'm not surprised – variety of opinion is a good thing.

But this then somehow translated into the BBC reports as 'Paganism has been recognised *by some* as a religion' (emphasis mine). So from The Druid Network getting a charity number to 'Druidry is a religion for the first time in 2,000 years', and then to 'Paganism = religion'. Look, here are some Real Pagans. And my social media Friends request pages go crazy...

Aside from the deeper meaning of 'Druid', 'Pagan' and 'religion', the story was visibly evolving before our eyes; from the initial decision announcement to the media involvement, to the responses coming in from anyone with an opinion (not just journalists). The announcer reading my name out on BBC News, and then seeing my name with the title 'Chaplain' beneath (I'm not) just exhibited the bizarre nature of storytelling, and how anything can be conveyed as 'true' if presented in the right way. My intention in saying 'Yes' to this lunacy was to emphasise that we, as active Druids, *are* out there to help people. The Druid Network as a charity is to be *of benefit to the community*. That is the point.

The BBC is not a tabloid. Many people believe it to be telling accurate and moderately unbiased reports of 'real life', and having heard first-hand from a BBC producer, they do try to listen to your own tale rather than twisting it – you're another licence-fee payer, after all. But even so, certain aspects of a story are more interesting than others. Druids should wear robes, for example, rather than jeans (although I did try). There is finite time to convey select information – as I said, hopefully people will go out themselves looking for more.

And so the point of this all... after the discussion, the debate and argument, the representation and misrepresentation. Despite the truth of the Charity Commission's report, it now seems that Druidry – and Paganism as a whole – IS a religion. *Because people are saying so.* Does this make me a chaplain, then, as ordained by the Broadcasting House of London, voice of the people of Britain? (joke!)

However, ultimately, isn't acknowledgement by the people the most 'official' recognition of all? And haven't I said this before – I'm called by folk, so I do my best for them. Does this need some sort of certification to be more true? Or is their simple 'Thank you' enough?

What this mad time taught me is the need for listening. The *need* for story that we all have.

The Bards used to hold the histories of the land, true enough. There are those who do that still, reflecting the stories as texts as well as the mood of the land at a particular time. But that's not what I mean.

Each of us tells our own unique story as we go through life. We may feel like we're not really getting anywhere day-to-day, but then when we stop to consider, looking back, we can see what we have actually accomplished. Even if it doesn't seem like a lot to us, just ask a friend, a family member or other loved one. A lot can be achieved in a quiet way, and we constantly tell each other the stories of those we've met (even if they might not recognise themselves in the telling!).

The media is looking for a quick synopsis of Druidry, a summary of What We Do, as if it were easy to fit entire individual and group philosophies of life into a small news 'story' sound-bite. When asked to make a public statement, I'm both very aware and very curious about how I come across, to individual listeners and entire demographic groups.

I'm telling just a *tiny* part of my story, trying to convey my truth, but aware that understanding cannot possibly be fully told in such limited space. There's no room for discussion, and the people listening... will not always be fully listening.

We don't, do we? Really *watch* the news. How many assumptions do you make about those subjects of each story? Politicians, celebrities, those famous for being famous. We have opinions based on what we are told, without considering *how* we are told it. Even when those people protest about their depiction, we simply adjust our opinions slightly and form new ones – probably no less inaccurate. Often, biographers and siblings of famous folk tell of the difference between the 'Name' and the 'Person' – as if the 'Name' is the caricature, the 'Person' hiding behind that public façade.

All stories are limited to the understanding of both the teller and the listener. So is this book. I've received wonderful feedback on my writing in the past, but am still amazed (and grateful) at how many actively make time to read it. Ultimately, I'm simply telling my tale, and hoping it comes across with true intention.

But that, to me, is a good healthy part of what Druidry *is*. It's not, and never has been, all about Stonehenge. The dressing up, the ritual, the calling of deity – they are all just parts that make up the tale.

The story continues to be told.

Living the Tale

I was once called to minister a funeral at the beginning of the week and a handfasting at the end. Two extremes. For the funeral, I met the widow and family two hours before travelling to the crematorium. For the handfasting, I had met the couple just a few short months before.

The relationship was formed through necessity in both cases. It had to be. Formed and evolved in a short length of time, the story surmised from what I was told, the rite tailored around this story – a crucial time of change to mark a memorable event (like it or not). I do my best to listen, to reflect the mood that is wanted, and to serve as best I can. That is my role as priest.

But it amazed me to see the different reactions to what was going on: people picking and choosing the parts of the story that they could understand best.

Sitting in the kitchen of a grieving widow, close family around. More and more people arrive, express their condolences... and then vanish outside, to chat and to smoke, to await the arrival of the hearse in readiness to form a procession. No rules for such an occasion, so waiting to be herded, told what to do and where to go.

I sit and listen, a relative stranger, the only mark of my priesthood the silver scarf over my dark suit. Priestess of Arawn today. But they know.

I listen, learning about this man who has passed and left such a mark that so many friends are here to see him off; that I might represent him well in a 20-minute slot at a crematorium to those who loved him. We chat. Stories flow.

Finally, it's just me and her. She tries to keep a brave face. The stories keep coming. And then, the simple clasp of a hand, holding her at a time when no other dares, in case she might shatter. Being there, holding the tale of her and her man, where he could not, and others didn't know how. Listening, with all of my heart and soul.

He's standing behind her, visibly heartbroken that he can't take her in his arms and give her comfort. He'd never want her to hurt so much, his lady. But then the stories turn to good times, of gifts and parties, drunken escapades, music and laughter. Those are the memories to cherish, the real story of who he is.

He nods and smiles with her.

A voice from outside, as the huge black car pulls up. "He's here."

Time to go.

***

Standing in a beautifully misty field one autumn morning, soaked with dew from ankle to knee, I breathe deeply. Fresh country air, wood-smoke, horses.

Guests start to congregate, picking their way through the long grass. The sensible – and brave – ones see my bare feet and kick off their own (now very muddy) shoes, laughing at the impracticality of 'proper' wedding clothes at such a time, in such a place. I try not to smile at the comments on the nice weather, the nervous glances as folk are unsure what to do, whether to speak to me or not. The madness of standing in a farmer's field, overlooked by ancient hills and curious wildlife, when we could be in a nice, warm building. What is this 'handfasting' lark, anyway?

The couple arrive, filled with joy, a sense of naughtiness and amusement at knowing what is to come. Living their fairy tale, dressed in their finery, children laughing as we all play together.

And then we begin... and the couple realise the challenges before them.

***

I stand before them all, staff in hand, ready to represent their wishes at this life-changing moment. I see the confusion on the faces of the regular folk. Some nod and smile, others are totally out of their depth.

And so I walk, before the coffin or around the marriage circle, weaving the tale of what we are doing, drawing them in.

Nobody is allowed to be passive at these rites. All bear witness, listening hard. A few gradually come to understand and relax; others don't. I tell the tale, hold the energies, listen and speak the truth of those present, in body and spirit. I guide and bear witness.

Those who are brave enough to speak to me afterwards all express their pleasure at 'how it went' – the picture that was painted, the story told. In that brief time, the marking of a monumental event will remain in the memory and be held close.

We move forward, together.

Our stories are about feeling the connection in a single moment and representing it as best we can. A tiny page in a life, a single day. All-important for some, just a duty for others.

So what are you, at any given point? A storyteller, a witness, a passive supporting artist... all of these or none? You stand in your truth, like it or not – so explore it. See how it sounds. Take up your courage and start on the next page.

If a microphone were shoved in your face *right now*, if you were called upon to speak of yourself or one you loved, what story would you tell?

Fire and Shadow

Samhain. A complicated time for pagans, full of questions and questioning, celebrating outwardly while looking deep inside. A liminal time, standing on the cusp of the future while holding sight of the past.

So let's do that. Answering that most common of questions: What do you DO on Halloween?

Last year. Gathering of the Hearth at my home, spending the day together building fire, questing for gifts for those who come knocking, considering the rite to come as the sun moves across the sky. Laughing with those on my local High Street as the energy rises, children keen to put on costumes and stay out late. The mood is clear and vibrant, the festival touching even those who don't know the meaning behind the pumpkins and skulls.

A last-minute call. Watching the final touches being put to the bonfire in the garden, punch being poured, merriment and madness, the wonderful smell of wood-smoke... as I stand in my kitchen, on the telephone to a national radio station with my mind half in this world and half in that of ritual. Trying to explain exactly what is going on in words that listeners can understand, finding it hard to believe that this is really happening. And then the call from my father 200 miles away: "So... what's this about being a Druid then?"

In the garden, flames licking high into the clear, cold night. Gate flung wide to admit any visitors who come... then all too soon, closed as we turn inward. Each with their own thoughts to let go from the past year, friends and family to greet in passing, promises to make, to plant in the dark earth. Everything I have goes into the rite, holding the space, holding the group, my beloved family in fur and feather. Standing together, in the only place we can be on this night.

***

A year before. Huddled in the woods. Another day of preparation, this time for a group ritual for strangers. The bonfire has been built, a path prepared, guests on their way. My partner and I sit on the cold earth by a thick holly bush as it starts to rain, protected by our cloaks but soon frozen by the fingers of the wind, soaked by the icy drops. We chuckle – how glamorous, this Druidry business!

And then we hear them, the visitors. Those who are brave enough to enter into the dark forest on this night, lanterns held high, unknowing of what they will find. The modern world seems far away right now.

We stand by the trees, watching, unseen, until the time comes to step out, painted and dripping. Facing those courageous few, themselves frozen in terror, challenges ringing out into the darkness.

"Why do you come here? Who's going to protect you? Aren't you scared? You should be..."

We take their lights away, separating the group. Each must face his own terrors, alone on the path this night. The spirit of the wood is strong, dancing, laughing at their fear. They cannot know how safe they are, how honoured for being there – but the challenge of the land isn't easy.

As we are challenged. The voice of the trees in my head, the darkness, the ancestors. The flames of the bonfire flicker against the doorway to the Otherworld, as it reflects nothing back. I look into the eyes of those around, seeing more than the friends I know so well, hearing the howl as they long to run free. The spirits are with us and within us. I wonder what they see in me, the wildness contained so tentatively in this strange body.

We vanish back into the trees. The guests are led to safety, drinks are opened, celebrations begun. We step up, war-paint removed as if back to normality. We are thanked, as if it were all a game. But the wildness is still there, in my mind.

Don't you know? It says. It's the everyday that's the game. You just experienced the real world.

***

And before. Months in preparation. Wearing only a long dark blue shift, on a day that has been noteworthy for torrential wind and rain storms. Miles from anywhere, the Island of Mona on the edge of the world. The road bridges have been closed until the weather calms, so there's no escape.

I wait to die.

I could claim that I was patient, meditative, prepared. I would be lying. The fear rose as the minutes ticked by, sitting along, waiting to be summoned. Much as I wanted to do something, anything, I dared not move. The future is uncertain. Nothing exists but this moment. Tomorrow is a world away... and it seems a very real possibility that for me, it may never come at all. Certainly not in any way that is familiar.

Finally, I hear the knock. It's time.

I step into the darkness, feeling the earth move beneath me – dense mud, sharp twigs pulling at my hair, icy rain on the face. And then a lantern. Voices. Taking me forward.

I am bound willingly. I stand tall, terrified but determined. I make my promises. I stand on an ancient stone as many have before me, feeling those who bear witness gathered around. I trust. And I die, three times.

Ritual, you think? You weren't there.

After, the smiling faces, the warmth, that life-sustaining British elixir that is tea.

Knowing that everything has changed. Don't be afraid to step into the darkness. Know that you are held.

The festival of Samhain celebrates the end of harvest, the beginning of winter. The clocks are turning, the leaves are falling.

Depending on the closeness of our connection to the world, we can feel it in our bones and our blood – but even those deeply immersed in modern city life can smell the wood-smoke on the wind, feel the chill in the air and dream of a little longer safely wrapped up in bed each morning. Our animal selves remember the urge to hibernate, and so now we feel the call to turn inwards, to review the year gone past and see what our harvest has brought. What will sustain us over the winter months until the next time of planting?

It is also the time to sit in the dark with those gone before. The ancestors are paying us a visit for a brief moment, and so it is only right that we be with them, honouring them and listening to what they may have to say. But this is not easy. Those same primal urges insist that we stay inside, in the safe warmth of familiarity. Turn the light on, comfort ourselves with easy distractions. We've got work tomorrow, we can do it another day.

No – we can't. This is the time. The world is turning and it does not wait. We are part of it, as we are part of our ancestral line. Protesting does nothing; we cannot reject our own blood. The darkness is as much part of us as the light, with the connotations of fear or safety being only those that we ourselves add, through the eyes of society and upbringing. The darkness contains so much potential, just waiting to be found. But to do that, we have to look.

If you walk this path with truth, honour and courage, you *must* walk it. This is your responsibility. Each has his or her own unique road of life, one that does not stop even if we must. After a while, we feel ourselves pushed forward – we make our vows, so our gods ensure we work to fulfil them. And we know, deep down, that we *want* to be pushed. We cannot stagnate any more in the sleepy ignorance that we once called 'normal'. We want to move forward, to learn... and to find, in our inspiration, that sometimes it's easier to run or even dance.

So we go outside. We feel the energies of the season, the beautiful unique light that is 'autumn' on those crunching leaves. The fast-approaching twilight, the starry darkness lit by bonfires. We come together as families, of blood and spirit, to share food and drink and to remember. To laugh and to cry.

Not so very different from the days of those same ancestors, who stood on this same earth before us.

If nothing else at Samhain, ask yourselves what you have accomplished over the last year (and beyond, if you wish). Feel the flow of life, of your path, as it winds into the future. What did you plant, all those months ago? How has your harvest been? What have you learned?

Where are you, right *now?* You stand here, today, this moment.

What are you doing?

Ancestry and Responsibility

Something that I was taught and like to pass along is the idea of our value as ancestors. As society is growing to (re)realise the importance of remembering those past, at specific times such as Remembrance Sunday, and for specific reasons – reaffirming our goals of peace and community over war and division, realising what we are leaving for those future generations of children yet to come – this is an ancient practice that needs to be relearned, for our connection as a species.

What have we learned from those gone before us? A common enough question, but one that's rarely explored fully these days. Of deeper interest within Druidry is how *well* we live our lives as directly honouring those who have gone before. Keen to move on with our busy everyday roles in the now, or looking to the future, it's easy to forget the reality of the past, and how quickly we ourselves are moving into it.

We are all ancestors. No matter how hard we may try, we cannot escape our blood and those who passed it on to us. This is not something that we can pick and choose. It's done, happened, certain, fixed. Going back generation after generation, each of our ancestors gifted us something, in genetics and in spirit – be they lords or barrow-boys, shopkeepers or explorers, murderers or prostitutes. Each was a parent, each a real person with their own lives, joys and fears.

We are the sum total of them, here and now.

Think about that. Consider for a moment the responsibility of that. Those of you with children, ponder how you would like them personally to remember you – and how (if at all) you'd like unknown future ancestors to remember you. As real people would be a good start, but what gifts do you send on down the years? What genetic challenges in your blood, or skills in your heritage do you offer for them to work with? This is a wonderful thing to be aware of, and an awesome responsibility – the least we can do is recognise it. But it's not easy.

While we focus on our families from a financial point of view – problems with pensions, legacies, childcare, or the cost of illness that requires round-the-clock attention – we all know that in our hearts, our families are far more than an intellectual exercise, to be quantified on a bank statement. Love them or hate them, they are part of our lives, as we are part of theirs.

Misunderstanding is inevitable, given the amazing variety of characters in the world. So how do we live with that, when we have no choice due to familial obligation? Do we overcome it, avoid it, or let it overcome us? How do our choices contribute to our story... and how will it read, when you look back? Perhaps your decisions are more understandable than you might think, especially the difficult ones. We all feel pain and joy. We can realise that, and help others as we have learned from our own lived experience and connection.

And so, my question continues: how are we living today? My constant harangue to those wishing to learn from me, asked so often it becomes boring, is 'What are you doing?'

Reading these words, obviously. Wondering what to have for tea. Wondering when this woman will get to the point.

No.

WHAT
ARE
YOU
DOING?

This is *not* a guilt-trip. This is not a religion telling you to suffer for the sins of those gone before, or an environmental plea to think of the world you leave behind.

This is the voice of someone shaking you roughly by the shoulders and forcing you to *OPEN YOUR EYES.*

Someone screamed and bled when you were born.

Someone died for you on a field in a foreign country.

Someone burned their clothing to allow your freedom of speech.

Someone worked until they went blind.

Someone made a decision that resulted in death.

It's easy to say we should be grateful. Indeed we should, but human nature makes it difficult to be grateful and give thanks to those we don't know – the idea's just too amorphous. Finding out names is a start, and creates a wonderful sense of connection as we see the family tree grow.

But what *is* possible is to live in awareness of this. Remembering one day a year is all very well, but do we really live as those who've gone before might have wished?

Without knowing specifics, again it's difficult. But it's not hard to make reasonable assumptions.

Sometimes the learning curve is tough. At several stages in my life, I've fallen and lacked the energy to get up (physically, mentally, emotionally, you name it). I'm still healing. We all go through this. But I've been shaken too, kicked hard in my complacency to get a move on and really, consciously *do*.

It's a beautiful summer's afternoon. I stand in the wood, alone on top of a small mound, enjoying the sound of birds and small creatures going about their business. My Grove-friends are nearby, setting up a picnic. I breathe deeply, wiggling my toes in the lovely thick grass.

The woman next to me has long, chestnut hair, and is dressed strangely. Her skin is dark from mud and sun, but her eyes are bright. She's surprised to see me here, but welcoming, glad. She has something to show me.

We walk together down the hillock, into a thick circle of trees that are somehow darker than the rest, as if burned. I look for evidence of a bonfire, but see none. Peculiar.

Then I hear the women screaming.

The tree-trunks are black, leaves skeletal. The ground is a marsh, deadly and cold. I can no longer see the sky, the air is heavy, darkness all around, the pain and sorrow...

I back away and run, just a few feet, but a world away. The sun is still high, the green canopy waving merrily overhead, squirrels jumping between branches.

I take a friend aside and tell him what I saw. His face becomes serious and he nods.

Later, we speak to a more experienced priestess who visited the site beforehand. She looks at me, just starting out on this path.

"You heard the women, didn't you."

The words cut through me and I can't speak.

The mound was a Bronze Age burial site for a tribal leader, long forgotten and unmarked on any modern map. The men of the tribe went away to fight, but they lost; those few who returned brought only corpses. And the women screamed.

So I learned to witness, and to remember.

The main thing that seems to put people off the Druid path is the essential requirement of Taking Responsibility and actually Living your life. That's as it should be. It's not an easy road. But we do the best we can.

My spiritual connections remind me that by *not* pushing myself, by allowing my skills to go rusty, letting myself whinge without purpose, avoiding responsibility, I am dishonouring both my gods and my ancestors, those who have been there for me when needed and always will be. I am ashamed by this, but also inspired – to get the hell up and *move*, to do something worthwhile, to find a focus and move towards it (even if that's the hardest thing in the world at that moment).

I honour my friends and my family. I honour my gods and my ancestors. I try to live well, to truly listen, see and speak my truth (never the easiest task), and to take responsibility for myself.

Sometimes it's too easy to apologise... far harder is saying 'No, I really *did* mean to do that' and dealing with the consequences. I promise to do my best, over and over – that's the best I can do, and I really mean it.

A dear friend once asked me what my secret was. 'Recently it's like watching someone wake up, seeing you getting on with your life and work.' We wake up every day. For that, we are blessed.

Now, what are we doing?

Moving onward.

Awen

So what is 'Awen?' There's a question. That intangible force, so intrinsic to Druidry as it is practised today. Hard to put into words, and often taken for granted or glossed over as a result.

Awen is the 'Fire in the Head' that made the Bards compose their immortal tales, including that of Cerridwen and Taliesin, the original brewer and taker of this tantalising elixir. Three drops inspired, any more would poison. The Romans then told of how it made the Ovates shake, their eyes black with visions. Awe-inspiring indeed.

I personally cannot imagine life without the touch of Awen, both from a Druidic and a general everyday perspective. I wouldn't be writing this book without it, compelling me to sit here every day and tap away ideas, ensure that I truly am saying what I mean intellectually and feel inside spiritually.

I also sincerely hope that everyone has experienced such a thing at one time or another (ideally on a fairly regular basis): a glorious 'Eureka!' moment, when your chosen muse speaks to you and creativity pours forth by whatever medium suits you best, be it acting, music, baking or gardening.

This isn't an adrenaline rush, by the way (although it can be). This is a moment of creative joy, where the truest possible expression of your own personal creativity comes to fruition. While normal life can then seem a little dull in comparison, the connection with Awen buoys you up through the knowledge of its constant nearness and tangibility… although there are those wonderful, mad creatives who make it their mission to seek it out directly.

The inspiration for this particular topic came from a fairly secular and everyday source: comedian Russell Brand (who clearly channels a good deal of energy into whatever he does). He sums up the sensation pretty well in his first biography.

Unfortunately, the description is in the negative, as he tells how it feels to *lose* that connection:

> 'What [Ritalin] was really like was severing the tendrils from the heavens that connect me to creativity. When I'm on-stage or on TV, and everything's going well, I feel like there are these electric, celestial tentacles dangling from on high and I can swing on them, like Tarzan on his creepers. But Ritalin severed those tentacles – just lopped them off.'[7]

I truly believe that as human animals, we *need* to create something in life, something tangible, for ourselves or to share joyfully. Some feel this urge more than others. To *not* feel this is a tragedy, and deep down, we know it. Especially those who numb themselves with poor substitutes like drugs (ironically, often due to their quest to actively seek out such sensation).

As I mentioned before, I once asked on a Druid-based forum what the relationship is that people have with Awen. To me at the time, it seemed to be something to aspire to, to endeavour to maintain that constant connection with inspiration. Kind of like the New Age concept of 'Enlightenment.'

The response I got was not itself very inspiring. Awen as a concept seemed to be more attractive and palatable than Awen as a tangible reality. Understandable I suppose, but my Druid practice was and is about actual connection, finding joy in the spirituality and RE-ality of an actual practice. Mental, philosophical ponderings are good brain-food, but they only go so far, after all. To truly *feel*, we must *do*. Awen is experiential, and enjoys being explored.

These days, I understand that maintaining a constant connection is not the best of plans – that way leads to madness, simply because we are not able to maintain such a state of being (see the story of Russell Brand again, perhaps). However, Druid practice, to me, intrinsically involves the ability to link to Awen, whether that is for you as an individual, or when leading a group. Energy work, the creative flow, the inspiration which is something that we work with and bring back into our daily lives, both personally and for others. We seek, learn and teach, through the results of our creative endeavours.

When an author writes, where do the tales come from? When a musician composes, where were those words before they were first sung? The classical concept of the Chorus, the Muses, those who create that spark of idea, the light bulb above the head – that's the experience of Awen. Light from above, clarifying the way.

In the darkness of winter, we look even more than usual for the creative fire that keeps us warm and nourished. Please ask yourselves: how are you finding your Awen in your life? And how are you sharing?

Modern Fairytales

Years ago, I wrote an article about the representation of paganism in movies and on television, with the rise in popularity of programmes such as 'Buffy the Vampire Slayer' and 'Charmed'. Since then, many scholarly books have been published dissecting our fascination with 'modern magic', but as witches, Druids and their brethren are stepping from fiction more openly into the mainstream, there have also been growing numbers of complaints by Real Pagans about how they are portrayed.

Since the original 'Witches of Eastwick' movie, pagan organisations have gathered to protest the 'truths' told in the mass-media, most commonly on grounds of religious discrimination and misrepresentation. I have no problem with this if the claim is well-founded; the internet certainly allows all of us a louder voice than we may once have had. But I've noticed that as with the above examples, even if the depiction of pagans is inaccurate, little real harm has been caused because these shows and films are clearly marketed as *fiction* – not newscasts, not documentaries. While the power of story has already been mentioned in these pages, I would argue that these fictions have in fact acted positively by inspiring real interest from viewers who may never have otherwise considered a pagan path. (The protests themselves may do more harm than good, but that's another topic for another day.)

While it's hard to believe sometimes, most intelligent people *can* tell the difference between movies and reality, although misunderstandings are perhaps inevitable when dealing with a topic so long taken for granted as magic. There's that old image of Getafix or Gandalf appearing in your head when Druids are mentioned, or the Wicked Witch of the West (or even Glinda the Good Witch, with her starry wand) for Wiccans. I've been told what a *good* role model Merlin is for those of us who regularly wear robes!

Rather than condemning the public stereotypes, it seems that we can now more easily see that movie and TV producers are actively considering the reality behind the mythology and incorporating it into their work – albeit a little changed, just enough to avoid those legal protests. Many teenagers came to Wicca through movies such as 'The Craft' or 'Practical Magic' (both fairly positive, upbeat and inspiring depictions), while 'Buffy' showed an extreme fictionalised version of what happens when magic is relied upon to live your life. Many authors who use paganism in their work are themselves active trained Priests, telling their truths couched in fiction, with the intention made clear that magic is only as positive or negative as the intention of the person casting the spell.

I've found the difficulty these days is often convincing people that I've *not* just watched one too many magical movies; that Druidry *is* a legitimate faith and way of life, and I myself *can* tell the difference between Oz and Kansas (one's sepia-tone, in case you didn't know). The worry of the conservative fringe that such media is negatively influencing the young is fairly redundant – the young will be influenced by *something*, that's just life and its quest for answers. Perhaps we should teach young people how to more effectively think for themselves?

So this is what happens when someone comes to me asking questions: I'll recommend them some books, ask what experience they have so far (usually including what movies they've seen), and once common ground is established, we can start to talk. I don't evangelise, but I'm happy to chat about what I do – it's then up to the listener to decide what they want to do next, and that, in its way, is the hardest part. Life, after all, is *not* like the movies.

I'm also pretty sure that 99% of the folk who come to me eventually decide to get on with their lives as before, once they've realised that I can't teach them how to shoot fireballs or create love potions, and that actual *work* is involved. I read a very good description of the process this week, referring to Witchcraft directly but equally true of most Pagan paths:

> '*As most practitioners of the Craft learn within a few years, [the] old magickal adage about not being able to speak of metaphysical or spiritual mysteries has little or nothing to do with the keeping of... Craft secrets, but reminds us that Witchcraft – or Wicca or any other sect of Pagan practice – is an* experiential spiritual path, *one we must undergo alone... Witchcraft is a religion for those with the tenacity of charging bulls, not for flocks of sheep waiting to be led.*[8]

People will always be searching – there are just more options these days to choose from.

Meanwhile, those of us who can tell the difference will quietly smile when asked the latest question based on 'Harry Potter' or 'Eastwick' – but at least be adult enough to try to point the curious in the right direction. Waving the appropriate type of wand, obviously.

Now, where did I put that golden sickle, there's some mistletoe wants harvesting...

Passion

Quite a few years ago, when I was taking my first steps into the world of Druidry, I had the immense pleasure of taking part in a women's sweat-lodge. This was in Oxfordshire, the heart of England in the heart of summer, and I'd taken time off work especially. My (rather confused, but curious) friends wished me luck.

I travelled up the night before with two ladies I had never met until then, sharing a ride and a vastly humid hotel room off the motorway, sharing our nervousness as it turned out that none of us really knew what we had signed up for. What was a sweat-lodge? What would we be asked to do? And… we'd have to be naked, right? Could we not even wear a towel?

The lodge was held in the grounds of a beautiful private house, that I have since had the pleasure of staying at many times. Nobody knew each other. A dozen women coming together, out of their daily lives on an otherwise normal weekend, getting involved in who knew what.

We built the lodge. We gathered wood and built the fire. We tried to prepare as best we could. We were terrified. All those women… we all thought it. What would they think of my bum, my stretch marks, my boobs?

The sun moved across the sky and at dusk, we danced. We drummed. We not only got naked, we madly painted each other with mud, marvelling at each other's differences, our forms and curves, the marks of our lives clear on our bodies. We crawled into the stifling dark space of the lodge together. And the world changed.

I crawled out again, minutes and aeons later, physically steaming. I screamed my soul out into the night sky. We all held each other and laughed, imagining staid Oxfordshire at night hearing our voices and wondering who was being murdered. I gazed at the bodies of the other women as they gazed at me, an array of beautiful shapes and lives, their fantastic smiles, the way they sang, the stories they told.

The next day, we returned to our homes, our 'normal' lives. I felt exhilarated, open in a way that I never had been before, bared before the world and the eyes of others. What can you do to me? I've danced naked in a field! (That was my mantra for some time afterwards.) It still makes me smile, when doing something exceptionally humdrum, such as standing on a crowded Tube platform in a busy city. How very un-English, what if they knew... who would be shocked? Who would be jealous?

My partner now tells me that on my return, I was glowing. Eyes bright, full of energy, I felt I could do anything – I was amazing in a way he'd never seen, radiating joy and life. My spirit was still dancing.

But as time moved on and normality returned, with the demands of those around taking over once again, he said that the difference became physically evident... and alarming. My shoulders slowly slumped to their previous level, eyes dulled, energy almost visibly drained off by others, until I was practically buried under the strain of so much pulling on me. As if others could not stand for me to be so bright; they had to take, to bring me back to normal levels with their demands (one even said as much). Or if I couldn't stand to be so open for long amidst what was my everyday life then.

Such an experience, however, is impossible to forget. I hold it in my heart still. That was one of many catalysts that changed my life, that allowed me to explore because now I had an idea of what I was looking for. I had felt it, and wanted to feel it again – and to share it with others, this chance to really be free, to be myself, to be wild and awed and awesome. To be rid of unnecessary pain and realise what fuelled *me*, what keeps me going, where my inspiration comes from.

The trouble is, that wasn't just an isolated incident, not just a weekend break that I could then add to an imaginary list of 'Things I Have Done'. The effect is still very much present, and it's bigger now. I've done more, have felt more, am proud of myself for accomplishing more. I know now when the notes of my life strike both true and false. My everyday life has changed immeasurably as a result.

When I'm drained by people or events that shouldn't have such power but do, it's because I can't help giving part of myself to them, in my efforts to help (I always have; I've been called naive often because of it). I have to battle, to move away or be subsumed... and I am coming to the inescapable conclusion that this means actively rejecting a good many parts of 'normal' life. Quite a bit of which I have already done, simply by questioning what is needed and what is not, but I am aware that even this prioritising places me apart; before we even get to the 'mad woman in robes' thing. I question. I search. I truly do try my best.

It is hard to find passion in daily life, but it is there. We know it is. Some don't like that knowing – it makes us too wild, too uncontrollable, too much of a threat. In truth, we *need* that wildness to live. I choose to be awake, not asleep. Even in times of hibernation, trapped at home surrounded by snow (as I write this), I'm still searching, bare feet against the frozen earth, then burying myself in warm places to consider, assess and (hopefully) prepare for what's to come. Whatever that may be.

Yes, it's terrifying. But it's more terrifying to know that you've felt such a thing and then actively worked to suppress it. To suppress it in others. To live in fear of feeling, of touching, of letting yourself live connected to those around.

How would you feel, naked in a field? How do you challenge yourself? What do you dream of doing, deep in your heart? Why aren't you doing it, or preparing for it? What are you afraid of?

We feel the wrongness and yet we live with it. Let's change that. It's incredibly hard, but that's life – and we have to live it unafraid.

Celebration

Many Pagan authors have written about whether Druidry is celebratory or not. On explaining the reasoning behind many pagan festivals and how they are observed in modern times, the questioner usually notes that paganism is a faith that sets a high value on celebration – and rightly so, it does. There are quite a few more festivals, for starters.

But if I may, I would like to clarify why I celebrate when and how I do. I've been asked a lot lately: 'So, do you celebrate Christmas? Oh, what's Yule?' and then on the back of that, 'Do you celebrate birthdays?' Let's take a little look at what this means. And why such questions are daft.

We (that is, twenty-first century folk of whatever stripe) *don't celebrate enough.* This is *not* a religious issue, but a cynical observation on modern life. Perhaps a certain English reserve is a factor here, but then we are only just starting to celebrate the patron saint of England in public, let alone a rite for children entering adulthood.

(For those overseas, England has recently realised that it has no patriotic national holiday, and there are calls for St George's Day to fit the bill. Previously it has either been forgotten entirely or generally agreed to be ignored, as celebrating it could cause offence to other nationalities. The British, however, are quite happy to celebrate St Patrick's Day, possibly due to the general goodwill of the Irish for anyone joining in with their copious alcohol consumption to toast a Dark Age Christian priest with a low tolerance for pagans, as opposed to celebrating a Syrian Roman who probably didn't fight a dragon at all).

The bizarre nature of what is 'tradition' is quite clear at certain times of year: lighting up the sky with your Christmas decorations is apparently fine (despite the immense bill and environmental consequence), as is spending money you don't have on gifts for those you hardly speak to, that they don't really want.

But I'll stop – this isn't a whining tabloid newspaper. I've been very glad to see that people are starting to question *why* they celebrate the traditions that they do, and actually looking a little deeper in an effort to make the winter festival more meaningful. More folk nod and agree when I explain why I don't send Christmas cards. Exclamations of 'what a good idea!' are prompted when my friends and I tell of how we make Yuletide gifts for each other to share together (while we don't mention the months of angsting over what to make and then swearing over the process itself in getting things right!).

The hilltop is dark, the streets lightly coated with ice. The air feels sharp against any exposed skin, tight in my lungs. My partner walks with me, to the highest point on the shortest day, witnessing the sunrise together on this Yule morning.

It's so cold that our hair is freezing with droplets of breath. Thick clothing doesn't help much. We hold each other, fingers firm through gloves and coats.

The light starts to change. The local creatures notice, as a blackbird suddenly announces his wakefulness to the new day with a brilliant burst of song. Cows slowly move between field and shed. A milk float trundles past.

It's a much slower change than the Summer Solstice. Colours graduate against the sky, as if their glow is fighting to break through the night. The planet moves, but so gently. We feel, as our ancestors did, that slight touch of dread – maybe this time, it won't happen? What if the sun doesn't come up? Imagine the perpetual dark of winter... that, then, is the message of this longest night. We don't just know it – we feel it cold in our bones.

Finally... there. At last. Our joy is tangible, the knowledge that we are witnessing something so (literally) everyday, but also the universe physically moving before us, with us as part of the process. The beauty of the changing sky, both the same and very different to that which our ancestors have themselves witnessed in centuries past.

We stand, as so many others have, remembering and watching, aware of our connection. To each other, to our families, to the land.

We return home, unable to stop smiling, and exchange gifts. The day is spent in celebration, with warmth, food and good company.

The sun has returned. The world moves on.

New Year (January 1st) feels awkward. Samhain is New Year for me; personally it makes more sense to see the annual cycle as the old year finishes with the final gathering of the harvest and 'closing down' of the summer days. I've never viewed the change in calendar as significant, especially with the early months of the year being some of the hardest in the run-up to Spring. Also, I've been at work for New Year, and it is by no means a time of universal celebration – just ask any Emergency Services personnel.

But I appreciate the turning cycle, as folk sigh and fondly wave farewell to the season of excess, moving forward into a time of resolutions, good intentions and new starts. We all do it every year, no matter when, and reviewing where you are in life (and where you are going) is a very good idea.

I think this is the key. We, as humans, *need* to celebrate, to mark changes in life. Paganism is particularly unashamed in this practice. Whether it's full or new moon rites, or particular festival days, we mark it somehow. Life changes (births, marriages, deaths and everything else besides) are made memorable, and in a truly sincere manner, with thought, care and attention. A handmade gift means far more than just a simple, cheap card. That and if done well, the creative act is itself a true pleasure!

We have become too cynical, too lazy, too much taking for granted the traditions passed down to us and forgetting the reasons that we practise them at all. Some need to be kept, some need to go (see above).

I do my best to mark the time in truth, as a Druid and as a human being. Others are doing likewise, trying their hardest to celebrate *properly*. I've been honoured to meet a fair few.

And *of course* I celebrate birthdays. We've survived another year! It's your own personal day, shared with others, but when friends and family remember what you've accomplished (good and bad). You're still going – well done!

Given what I said above about New Year, I once found myself chatting to a pleasant old gentleman who stood outside a shop in the cold, collecting money for a wildlife charity. As it came time to go, I wished him a 'Happy New Year'. He looked genuinely touched, and answered likewise. How many would just pass him by? How many of us are tired after all the effort of Christmas – did any of us even touch on the seasonal joy that we're supposed to be feeling? We mark things in our own manner. Let us not be dictated to or be afraid to do things 'our way', but let us remember, and share with those around in good heart.

Another example, if I may. Like everyone, I've heard a fair few Christmas carols, both modern and traditional. How many sound like they are *truly* celebrating? Words alone do not make for sincere praise. 'Tidings of comfort and joy' have become a dirge, and some carols just make no sense at all, despite their famil-iarity. From the looks on singers' faces, they are being sung 'because they should', and most are heartily sick of them by (or well before!) December 26th.

To be fair, pagan chants are actually not much better. Those pseudo-religious tunes sung in a minor key sound more like medieval Church hymns of apology and self-abasement than songs of happiness. The very late great pagan author Isaac Bonewits summed it up very well:

The Generic Pagan Chant
A-minor, D-minor, A-minor, D-minor

This is another Pagan chant
You can tell that it's real old
'cause it sounds just like a funeral dirge.
A-minor, D-minor, A-minor, D-minor
A-minor, D-minor, A-Flaaaaat!'[9]

I've said it before, no doubt I will say it again. Why are we doing what we do? If we stop and consider, can we not do it a little better – if it needs doing at all? And if you can't do something properly, why *are* you bothering? 'Because I should' is no reason at all. You must feel *something*.

To me, Druidry is indeed celebratory, in that it encourages *life* to be celebratory. We notice, we mark, we remember. Life is tough, despite all the modern luxuries we may have (and aspire to as gifts) – why should we be too proud to give a cheer? What are we afraid of?

My best wishes to you all at this time and every other. The sun returns as the days grow longer – I promise, I've seen it. I raise a glass with those I love, and suggest that you do likewise in your own way.

Create your own Traditions and move forward. You can be certain that others will be with you.

To Ignore or Inform?

In this modern, technological futuristic world that we live in (bear with me), I've spoken before of how appearing in public wearing robes and calling oneself 'Druid' seems to invite a certain response. I'd expect it to be similar for our friends in pointy hats, the Witches – and have indeed seen it to be so, with vocal Christian protesters outside the annual pagan conference 'Witchfest' in Croydon, Greater London. Although, interestingly, nobody ever seems to protest against Morris Dancers.

Without wanting to go into the difference between the two traditions, it has been suggested that the Witches have it worse. Druids were, and are, perhaps somewhat more respected as a scholarly group, historically made up of intellectual fellows who haven't threatened anyone since the Romans (and that was very definitely provoked). But the mental picture of 'Druid' is not as threatening as that of 'Witch', the associations are not so dramatic as the lone woman in black, in her cottage with her cat, something bubbling on the stove… yes, that's a description of me, right here and now. Clearly a threat to us all, with my subversive mutterings.

A friend of mine asked me to discuss 'how to be a Witch in modern times', given this stigma still attached to the label and, to be frank, I would be surprised if the majority of those reading have not experienced a similar reaction at some point in their training, as they come 'out of the broom closet'. She has found it awkward to use the term, despite it being the best descriptor of what she does, finding the word 'pagan' brings a less hostile response – despite the latter incorporating the former path into its umbrella of meaning.

Now, she obviously doesn't live her life wearing a pointy hat and getting to work by broom. None of us live the fiction. So why, when you have cause to discuss your spirituality – a very personal and usually deeply considered topic – is that image somehow superimposed over our actual selves? And how should we respond, if at all?

Joking aside, as I've said before, I've been very glad personally to find that the vast majority of those who approach me to talk about my Druidry do so out of curiosity. Why am I acting that way, what am I doing, why am I dressed like that. People aren't afraid, nor hostile, but interested. I can't tell you how wonderful this is to me (if a bit confusing, to be approached by random strangers!), as I do often expect a certain mockery or disinterest – or to quote Kris Hughes, Head of the Anglesey Druid Order: 'Ooh, look at that tit in a robe!'

But it does happen. While you don't go around in daily life dressed up and announcing to all and sundry that you're a Witch/Druid/Heathen/Christian/Jew, it can and does come up. I've been asked in a chip shop, 'How come you know so much about Halloween?' I find it best to judge the situation, assess how much information the person is actually looking for, and inform them accordingly; especially in a working environment where you then have to encounter that person every day thereafter.

Not everyone is looking for the Complete History of Paganism; some are just asking a simple question. Nor is everyone going to run for flaming torches and pitchforks if you answer honestly and intelligently (and not aggressively).

I consider myself blessed to live in a country where free thinking is largely encouraged and diversity is celebrated (to a greater or lesser degree). Even today, there are many places where calling yourself any of the names above would result in a much tougher response, if not beating or death. But you can't naturally expect to announce yourself as *anything* and expect immediate full understanding. That's part of the responsibility and challenge of diversity.

The Druid Network (to take an example I'm very familiar with) was set up specifically to encourage the facilitation of information about Druidry: what it is, what we do. Rather than saying 'this is our/my way', it is a group of like-minded individuals who work together to create understanding. Many other pagan groups do likewise. Although it's only in recent decades that pagan-minded folk have really been able to talk seriously to the wider world, gently but firmly advising that we are serious, not figures of fun play-acting at magic.

With the Charity Commission's decision to recognise The Druid Network's definition of 'religion', the national Census PaganDASH project (a drive to get Pagans counted correctly on the UK Census), international Pagan Pride events and suchlike, people are talking – including the mainstream media – and so others are listening and learning. Given the sound-bite nature of our culture, it's not always easy, and folk inevitably get things wrong; to be expected when discussing fairly amorphous and varied ideas, and given the lack of written text or dogma in paganism generally. This is compounded by the current nervousness of discussing spirituality within our rather sternly secular culture.

The media can help if we approach it responsibly, representing ourselves and our fellows accurately, but in ways that those entirely ignorant of us can understand (so no pointy hats, even in jest). If people see Druids in ritual on the BBC (that most respected of news media institutions) on Halloween, the connection is made between what is shown and what you – their colleague or sibling – do. The mental picture is adjusted slightly; the way is open for discussion.

But, similarly, this has also provoked hostility, albeit in a minority. The ignorance shown in right-wing newspaper opinion columns has been shocking and not a little scary... but sadly reflective of those who do not celebrate variety of belief in whatever form it appears. Ignorance leads to fear, which leads to kicking out, to remove the object of that fear and restore 'normality.' It is hard to discuss anything with such folk, without the shared intention of finding common ground. Equally hard is not reacting in kind, shouting similar unconstructive and aggressive abuse that just reinforces the criticism of pagans in general.

So what do we do? Keep quiet, get back in that closet? Or trumpet our beliefs from the rooftops, clad in purple velvet and waving a huge crystal wand?

As I said: common ground. We are all human, real people with beliefs in the world around us that were formulated (and are still evolving) to help us understand what's going on day to day and get through this thing called life. This includes atheists – science is that most fascinating of doctrines that we all subscribe to at some level. It's just important to remember that one path does not exclude all others.

When you are ready to call yourself *whatever* it is that you have decided you are… are you ready to *live* it? For the questions that will follow? Are you informed and able to talk about your life and beliefs? Not evangelise, in any sense – just simply explain, at a basic level, diplomatically and clearly? If not, I'd suggest keeping quiet a little longer, until your understanding and experience are greater. People *will* ask things you never ever anticipated. You *will* be flummoxed. Are you able to admit your ignorance and keep learning? Because that's life. It isn't a fad with a dress code and accessories.

Once you feel able, and a particular issue strikes you hard, take action with honour and integrity. Write letters, join multi-faith groups, instigate discussion. Promote understanding, which means talking at the level of your audience. Make friends with those who question; try to understand their confusion when they look at you. Don't take yourself too seriously, but gently explain the reality behind the fairytales – that's often far more interesting.

Do what we're all doing: live your life as the best Druid/Witch/Heathen that you can. That's the best advertisement for a way of life, after all.

Although pointed hats are fun at specific times of year.

My solicitor looks at me, smiling. She's been so supportive, helping with the legalities of my divorce, but aware of the quiet suffering that goes on behind the official process. Now is the moment, the final confirmation of my wish to separate from one I loved for so long.

A representative of the Court has arrived with the necessary paperwork. He'll be taking away my marriage certificate, that paper I was so proud of, never to be seen again. He's holding a small book.

"Are you OK to take the oath...?"

What?

"You have to swear under oath that what you say will be the truth."

He holds the book out to me. It's a King James Bible.

Something jolts inside me, but I can't help the small up-swell of laughter that threatens to spill out.

"I'm not Christian."

"Oh!" He's shocked, and a little embarrassed. "I can go back and get something else... are you Jewish?"

"No. I'm Pagan."

"OH!" Real alarm, now. "I don't think we have anything for that..."

My 'Professional Priest' takes over. "There is a Pagan oath, the equivalent of 'the whole truth and nothing but the truth.' But don't worry."

I take the Bible and place my hand gently on its worn surface.

"I swear that what I say will be the truth."

I pause, searching for the right words. Goddess, help me...

It's all right. Just speak.

I look into the clerk's eyes. "While I don't follow this book, I recognise the authority that you place in it and the intention and meaning behind it. So I swear by it and by my gods that what I say will be the truth."

There.

Both of them stare at me. My solicitor's smile grows wider.
Nicely done.

I've spoken of how finding paganism is akin to finding a name for something you've always felt, the feeling of connection to the natural world, that powerful feeling when seeing a sunrise, for example.

One response to this has been that many people feel that way, but that doesn't make them pagan. No, true – but we all have that undeniable connection, to each other in experience and (inescapably) to the world around.

I told this once to a curious work colleague, who sat nodding as I talked, clearly listening, but then responding with how she couldn't possibly do 'what I do' because of 'what people will think'. She went on to say that she doesn't even dress up to go out any more, after receiving harassment in the past from both men and women (she's young and pretty), but while she's learning to stick up for herself, she prefers to stay quiet, not creating trouble. She could never be handfasted, although it sounded lovely, because of 'what Mum'd say'.

I've been there – we all have. Why do we choose to stop questioning, to accept that world at our own expense? Is it for self-protection, or is it through fear of what might happen if we speak up? It's something I've always wondered. At what point do we make the choice to give up... or learn to fight back?

Sometimes it's hard to feel the joy in life, but the dark at least teaches priorities – what I definitely *do* want, compared to what I definitely do *not*.

I am determined to actively live my life, with all the difficulties that entails as I react to the normal everyday culture with both amusement and frustration. As I do, I am surprised to find the number of people who are brave enough to ask questions, then nodding and actually *agreeing* with my reasoning... before telling me why they could never do the same. I'm not asking them to – I'm simply suggesting that they live on *their* terms, be curious (as they clearly are, having approached me!), to seek out what they want rather than just settling for the easy option. Especially when that means accepting experiences that are actively detrimental and debasing, a decision that they will most likely regret deeply.

This is a difficult challenge, I know. But life is short. If you don't follow your dreams now, when will that time come – or when will it have passed you by? Are your goals held so close for your own sake or someone else's – and how much *will* you regret, when you stop and look back?

So, do you walk with honour and truth… or do you just stand still, eyes tight shut and fingers blocked into ears?

And if you see people standing like that, how much do you try to shake them – gently, but firmly, whispering: 'Wake up – you're dreaming…'

Do you just pass them by, comfortable in your superiority? Or just afraid of what they might say?

This is why I talk publicly. If I even inspire one person to look a little deeper to help themselves, it will have been worth it. I can't stop now, knowing that, always hoping...

If asked, I answer. I hope my tales convey a little of what inspires me as I muddle forward on my own journey.

Our Sexual Nature

One of the things that always seems to be mentioned whenever Paganism is spoken of in the media is the... well, let's just say the 'free love' practices. The skyclad Wiccans, the Crowley-style orgiastic gatherings, the Dennis Wheatley bloody sacrifices; it quickly enters the realms of lurid fiction. Ignorant readers are titillated, genuine Pagans are frustrated.

I will say at this point, if you're under 18, please feel free to *read on*. Because you will anyway, and I'm not going to be talking about anything particularly shocking (sorry, adult readers). Plus, censorship simply makes people look more keenly for whatever it is they're being told *not* to look at – and frankly, there's nothing here that shouldn't be talked about. Quite the reverse.

Sex is important to pagans, in the same way that it's important to humanity as a species. Family is at the root of community and connection, our ancestral lines would not exist without it, and an act that creates so much joy (if undertaken correctly) should be lauded, not stifled.

Aspects of Deity that are frequently incorporated into our lives and practices are the Great Mother, her Consort and her Son, amongst other archetypes. The fecundity of the land is represented well in the rampant enthusiasm of the priapic Pan and the engorged Sheela Na Gig; even the language is sensual, thick and intriguing, dripping with intention.

So it's remarkable that when discussing sexuality in pagan life, there's remarkably little information. Especially when we consider that according to the 'Mind, Body & Spirit' shelves in your local chain bookstore, the most popular spell that anyone could ever want is the Love Spell. That's an industry in itself and not an entirely ethical one.

If love spells were used to the extent that they're written about, the issue of 'controlling' others for the purpose of relationship can both be compared to – and result in – rape. The sheer invasiveness is precisely what modern Pagan practice is *not* about. If you're playing with the lives and emotions of others in such ways, you need an entirely different kind of help.

If undertaken with clear intention between two informed and consenting partners, love magic can be a powerful thing. From setting the scene for a night of passion as an expression of love for your partner, to invoking the spirits of fertility with the goal of conceiving a child, these are fundamentally human experiences. By making the occasion sacred, almost ritualised, not only will you have a memorable time (I won't say night, as this could happen at any hour), but you'll both experience connection at a much deeper level.

The power of sex is an almost tangible energy – and not just the act itself. Sexuality as a practice is a much more familiar concept, in its way. We're constantly being bombarded with images of it, and are tacitly aware of it in everything we do. Clothing and adornments are chosen to increase personal attractiveness, make-up exists in almost infinite variety to create human peacocks showing off on Friday nights in town centres. Without the subtle language of sex, many advertisements would be dramatically different. So how are we using that ourselves (and do we even realise)?

However, perhaps it's our essential 'British reserve' or a holdover from the rules of the larger faiths, but it seems to me that the reality of sexual relationship is still rather taboo within Paganism. We're all aware of the increased importance of woman (particularly in Dianic practice, for example), but the inclusive and comparatively open nature of the (wide range of) Pagan paths means that there are those from the entire sexual spectrum out there on Beltane. Heterosexual, homosexual or transsexual, we all understand (to a greater or lesser degree) as a crucial part of our spirituality that our actions represent both our personal power and that of our gods... as we participate in what is, at heart, possibly the most natural of all acts.

And of course, this isn't just the missionary position. A multitude of human experience can be brought to bear in the coital ritual, from the simple (!) expression of love to joining through a mixture of pleasure and pain or control games. Again done correctly, BDSM is not simply a dressing-up party, and it would be insulting to consider it so.

There are more ways of life, spirituality and relationship than I could possibly name here. Some Pagans are polygamous. Others abstain as a personal act of sacrifice. Many realise that gender itself is fluid, playing with the boundaries of clothing, identity and public image. The key word, again, is *consenting*. We should endeavour to understand, not judge.

As I've said before, when we act honourably in our lives on this path, we act with clear intention, knowledge and responsibility. If we surrender ourselves, that is a true gift to our lover. A candle-lit dinner is an act of worship.

And then, of course, there is the Great Rite... but that's another topic for another day.

Suffice to say, we are almost duty-bound as practising Pagans to welcome the act of love, to explore it and revel in it, as our gods do. If you're not enjoying it, why not? What can you do differently? Be curious, investigating together *with* your partner. The focus and goal is relationship, the joining of forces, merging and separating in natural rhythm, like waves on the beach (both forceful and gentle).

This includes, of course, self-love. From confidence and presentation to personal, private pleasures – such lone rituals are likewise to be made memorable and enjoyable. You should hold no secrets from yourself, after all. If you are God/Goddess, take time to worship!

Not to forget, finally, that ultimate Pagan sexual experience. If you're brave enough... get outside into the world! Wild nature is itself a sensual experience, from the feeling of sunlight on bare skin or wind through hair, to dancing in a torrential rainstorm or merging with the tickle of sand on a beach. Alone or with others, take time to open yourself and experience that fundamental relationship as you remember that whether wild or controlled, you are still an animal.

Live with awareness, live with joy, live with love. Especially on the long winter nights...

Why Are You Doing This?

So to continue the topic of how to live as a Pagan in regular society, the other common question I've been asked is: 'How can you be socially accepted as a Witch/Druid?'

My immediate response (perhaps rather annoyingly) is: 'You can't. Why would you want to?' Always with a smile – I've little clue of what 'social acceptance' really is, nor why we should aspire to it.

More helpfully perhaps, my reply should be: 'Ask yourself: Why are you doing this?'

These days, it's hard to be socially accepted by everyone, no matter what you are: a goth, a housewife, a Conservative Party member. You can't please everyone, and there will always be someone who wants to find fault.

But why are you, yourself, *wanting* to make the decision to identify yourself as a Witch/Druid/Heathen/Pagan? Is it because it seems 'cool?' Because it's alternative and interesting? Or because it truly is a title that most accurately reflects your own values and way of life?

Because as soon as you start talking about it, you *will* be asked to justify yourself. Which leads to my next question: 'Are you doing this for other people?'

I've seen a lot of Pagans quite obviously playing up to their perceived self-image or title for the benefit of those around. That's fine, provided they realise that it's generally a) playing dress-up and b) going to provoke a certain response. As I said before, be prepared to laugh at yourself before you start and you'll be fine.

Without at all wishing to appear derogatory, however, are you doing this for *yourself* or for *others?* By which I mean are you practising for the betterment of your life personally, or looking to work more within the community? Both are entirely valid, but very different in meaning.

If you're serious about your spirituality, a point will come when your practice as a Pagan (of whichever stripe) becomes your way of life. It will be so integrated into your world that the practice is almost entirely natural, not an activity separate from your work, your family, or anything else. You *are* a Druid (or Witch, etc.). This is not special or different, it's just a part of who you are. Many novices aspire to this – and it is a good goal to aim for.

But living as a Druid *doesn't* mean that you've reached some ultimate Enlightened Way of Being, after which everything becomes easier because you've found some secret spiritual knowledge. Your practice will still need to be maintained. As you move forward, so does your faith. It must constantly be changing, evolving and working *with* your life so as to remain relevant – otherwise we're back to that old question of 'why are you doing this?' At which point, you must ask yourself again: 'Who are you doing this for?'

I understand that the entire focal point of some modes of religious practice *is* to achieve enlightenment of some sort. That's not Paganism, and certainly not Druidry. It's a constant. You are, in a sense, continually being enlightened – as you practise, you learn. You are continually waking up each new day with new experiences and perspective, healing the past and moving forward with new potential into the future. That's active and rewarding life, continuous inspiration that you use personally and share with those around by your expression of it.

Which is fine, as far as it goes. If that's enough for you, lovely. Life is complex, there's a lot going on in it – more than enough to handle by one person in one lifetime!

But there is more, should you wish it. In other traditions, it may be a calling or vocation, but it's that time when practising purely by yourself is not enough. You want to work with others. Or *for* others.

Initially, this may be for personal reasons. A group to learn with is wonderful, sharing the journey together, and validating your own experiences. A light is brighter when made up of many flames.

Or you could be called upon to *truly* be Pagan 'for other people' – to serve as Priest. You may not have 'completed' your training (when have you ever?), but you want to be there *for* others, to help when called upon, whether they are actively seeking their own way or simply looking for information.

If any of these situations were to happen to you *today*, right now, would you be prepared? Are you ready? Do you know what you're going to say when asked those difficult questions?

Nope – you're wrong. You can't ever be prepared for *every* eventuality. But you can be strong enough in yourself to admit this and move forward anyway, still learning within yourself and *with* those who seek you out, who work with you, or who are just simply a bit interested.

Are you able to speak to people on the level at which they are ready to hear? It's not easy. Paganism is not an evangelical faith, and not everyone is ready to hear about the higher levels of cosmic reality before they've even fully absorbed the idea that the Christian God isn't the only deity out there. Some are shocked that we won't do magic to order, Harry Potter-style. Instead, we can tell them – and show them – what we *are*, and what we do, as truly Living Pagans (of whichever path). It's then up to them how to react and move forward. That's the closest to 'socially-accepted' practice that we can get.

A perfectly normal autumn morning. I navigate through the busy traffic, driving up to the school gates and inside, looking for a parking space. My partner and I step out of the small car and prepare for work.

The gasps from around are clearly audible. Two adults, dressed in robes and cloaks, gathering up a drum, a wolf-skin and a tall, ornately-carved staff... in the school playground!

We head inside and are instantly surrounded. Questions from every direction, mostly about the wolf-skin ('Is it real?' 'What's his name?' 'Can I stroke him?'), but occasionally 'Why are you here?' We answer honestly – the children are clearly bright and curious – before heading to the teachers' lounge.

A different level of questions, here, and some mild jokes. Just as interested, fortunately, and very glad that we're here.

It's multifaith day at a small country school. The Buddhist monk has failed to arrive, so we're the only ones in 'official regalia'. We ask our questions too – I'm fascinated by the Jain practitioner, not knowing much about his faith, and we swap stories enthusiastically.

We then take classes for the day, explaining what we do and (mostly) answering questions. From children of 12 to older teenagers, they're openly fascinated; we're constantly challenged, finding the words to explain what we do, to many whose frame of reference begins and ends with magic in fiction and on television.

Someone asks if we wear normal clothes. Of course!

'So why aren't you wearing them now?'

I ponder for a moment.

"If you had someone standing in front of you talking about Druidry wearing robes, or someone wearing jeans, which one would you be most likely to listen to?"

He thinks. "Robes, like you are."

I smile. "That's why."

In case they don't believe me, at the end of the day we change back into our 'normal' clothes. Most of them don't recognise us, with double-takes all around. But my smile stays in place.

They were listening.

Why are you doing this... It's something that I ask myself daily. I never *ever* believed I would be 'ready' to work in service to others, to accept the responsibility of the tasks asked of me, and be able to stand before my Gods and declare my truth in such work. Which (hopefully) is a good reason for me to do it.

I keep challenging myself, as others challenge me. I don't have all the answers, but I'm willing to have a crack at the questions and keep smiling. To fall down and get up again, with a hand out to help others likewise.

Do what you are comfortable doing, but please, be sure – or as sure as you can be. If it's the right path, you'll know it. If not, expect a cosmic kick. You'll find your way eventually.

And if not, there may just be someone you can find to ask.

Croxden Abbey, Staffordshire. Mid-morning, steady rain pouring from thick grey skies. I kick my shoes off into the corner of what was once a monk's dormitory, feeling the echo of stones under the thick grass beneath my feet. Just a few people present in body, intimate and close, nervous but resolute and excited.

As I begin to speak, I feel others gently peeping in, listening, curious. They've not been part of such a thing for many years, but ritual is clearly ritual, no matter what faith, and while the ground has been desanctified, those who lived here for so long have stayed on the land they knew best. We're not in the main building – that would be too intrusive – but I speak with awareness, and feel approval resonating at my words. The promises made may be in new words, spontaneous, unprepared, but they are heartfelt and familiar to any who have known what it is to join and be joined. I am merely the conduit. The two before me are the focus. Together we all weave their binding gladly and with joy.

Tintagel, the cliffs overlooking an ancient castle. A beautiful, bright day heading fast towards sunset. Fierce sea winds warn us to take care with every step, surrounded on three sides by the ocean with hidden paths ending in sheer drops. A great stone sits before me – apparently used before by film-makers to hold Excalibur. All it's missing is a lion.

Just the four of us here, the couple led carefully down the almost-path, having travelled so far for this moment and determined not to fall. Everything about this place is strong, determined and ancient. We bow to it and make our calls.

This is no polite public ceremony. This is a passionate yelling out, to the sea, land and sky, to the ancestors who watch, in words both familiar and strange. Promises are made in a language unknown to me, but with clear intention in the eyes that is absolutely familiar and always wonderful to behold.

I feel the presence of personal deities, theirs and ours. One unexpected... but then I look around me and smile. Not so unexpected, when you think about it. Wildness is key today. England is not always polite or quiet; beneath that everyday veneer lies unrestrained boldness, with laughter and honest truths that are hard to escape, especially at times like this. We stand before the ancients as we truly are, and are blessed.

Morecambe Bay, Lancashire. I love the different 'feel' of each part of the country as I travel, from the Romanised civilisation of Sussex to the busy weight of London... to here. Crucially North. But always the seaside promenade is familiar, with the scent of salt and chips, horses and dogs bounding on the beach, people out to walk despite the sea breezes and threatening rain.

No ceremony today, just a simple meeting of total strangers, preparing to bare their souls with strange words that 'normal' people don't use... but loving every second. No wedding-planners here, just clear intention and how to portray that. Building the ceremony from thought to reality.

I'm very glad that of those I've met by ritual, I've stayed in touch with almost all, as lasting friendships are made with like-minded folk. We have similarities and differences, but I'm often overwhelmed to be meeting such a mad mix of individuals – truly wonderful people that I'm proud to know. Within five minutes, I know that these fit into that category easily. In the coming months, we'll prepare... and then a sudden mad flurry of energy as the day itself hoves in sight. We promise to do our best, as always. That day will be both magical and memorable.

One thing all of these events has in common. The smiles on the faces of those involved are absolutely sincere, soul-felt and impossible to remove. The shining connection, between partners and friends, is a tangible web, a glittery cat's-cradle that will be there wherever they go as they move forward in life. Those who bore witness will keep that in their hearts – they have been part of something that reached deep into bone and spirit, stopping the universe to focus on their tiny part for just a brief moment... we always say this, and of course it's presumptuous. But it's no less true. Stand there with me in that moment and tell me otherwise.

So those were the weekends of February 2011. Missing out, of course, the many miles of driving, soulless motorway service stations, organising pet-sitters, hours of preparation (including worry over anything that we may have forgotten to bring), ever-present stage-fright nerves... I do always promise to do my best, but I have high standards. Awareness of the significance of each day is paramount in my head, and I truly do *do* everything that I can to (in work parlance) 'exceed expectations'.

And then the return to normality afterwards. Back to the everyday: work shifts, food shopping, walking the dog, helping a friend move house.

This isn't as clear-cut a division as it might seem, time-wise. We definitely are *not* 'weekend pagans'. Each week I have many calls and emails on a huge amount of varied topics, and I'm aware that being so busy at the weekend means that it's hard to keep up, but again I do my best. Advice on multifaith issues, potential legal issues with children at public pagan gatherings, a funeral vigil... and fairly often, chatting to a curious colleague about 'What Paganism Is.'

Not to forget my personal life. I'm not always 'on stage', available to anyone. I am happy to help when I can, but there have been dark times too – far too many for my liking in recent years. I walk often with a black dog by my side, and sometimes he jumps up to crush me. It's times like that when faith should sustain me, but those periods are usually the most challenging, when it's hardest to see through the fog obscuring every sense. I'm fortunate in having a loving partner, understanding friends and for life to generally allow me time to recover and move forward, but it's not easy. Working with your darkness is a constant battle.

I've found that since I have made the decision to intentionally work with my spirituality as part of daily life, my priorities have shifted dramatically. I find it almost intolerable to bear certain aspects of mundane life that previously I took in my stride, the petty injustices of the normal world, the hidden wrongness. Part of my training was to 'be curious', in every aspect of life, and so I do – but this has consequences. I've sought out and studied Environmentalism, and cannot help but probe deeper into rabble-rousing news stories to seek the truth of a tale (as well as why the media chooses to enhance certain aspects over others). Ethics and philosophy fascinate me, why people act in the way they do, how we as a culture ignore so much of life in this world.

Supermarkets and shopping malls make me physically ill; those enclosed spaces with no natural light and recycled air. Jeans for £5... wrong on so many levels. Casual abuse daily at work from those I am trying to help (both the public and fellow 'professionals'). So many people are trapped in their boxes, in their heads, knowing no way out let alone trying to seek it. But... I've been there too.

I do my best, as I've often said – to live *my* life now, with priorities that have come about for good reason, watching the pointless fall by the wayside. I still find myself caught up in the to-do list every day (who doesn't?), but it's when I'm close to collapse that I am forced to remember to recharge, to step outside, to simply *stop*. It's hard to avoid the hamster-wheel aspects of modern life, but this is the time when we realise how important it is to really *live*.

It's these times when I remember back, to any one of the

meetings, rituals or little chats when folk act with honour, truth and courage to change their lives, even a little bit – and have asked me to be there.

When I sit down to write this story, sometimes the words flow, sometimes they don't. I read back and think 'how on Earth will people take this?' Once out there, in the world, it's open to any. I bare my soul, expressing my truth as best I can, and cross my fingers for understanding, knowing that there will always be some who just think I'm a poser, trying to make myself look good by writing New Age rubbish. But at least I'm doing *something*. I constantly question my intentions and try to keep moving.

And so it continues.

As my original promise said: Step, step, step. Onward.

I'm sitting here pondering what to write. Aware more and more strongly of the background noise in my head, like the repetitive beat of a railway train, that says: 'I'm so tired'. A long day at work, lots of house jobs, pet sorting and emails replied to. I'm typing this on my laptop in bed. Because while yes, I'm tired, I still want to write.

I'm always honest here. Why would I not be? I know that my words will be read by many, mostly strangers; that I could make up a persona and people would believe it, so why not make myself better? Aside from the obvious 'because I'll get caught out when I fall flat on my face' (or because nobody enjoys reading total rubbish), I can only promise that I'm *always* writing from the heart. I promised myself I would when I started this journey, and it would be truly dishonourable to start lying to you all now. I have no reason to – my name is clearly visible on the cover and I respond when questioned. Neither superhuman nor infallible, just doing my thing.

Life asks a lot of us these days. I have no way of knowing if it ever didn't, but in recent months I found that I had somehow put my money where my mouth was. If I'm doing something, I'm really *doing* it. Properly and fully, true in intention and deed. If I catch myself doing a half-a*sed job, I try to yank myself up, give myself a shake and either do it properly or stop.

However, this has interesting consequences. Whereas in previous years, I've pretty much gone on and on, like the famous marketing icon of the Energizer Bunny, working hard until I completely run out of steam, I'm finding that my boundaries now have grown closer. I use up a lot of energy doing what might be considered 'regular, everyday' tasks, and then can't do other things (just as or even more important) because I simply don't *have* the energy, so can't undertake them – because I would not be putting everything I could into that job.

Let me make it clear, I'm not making excuses for *not* doing things. Some tasks can wait, but rarely indefinitely. Others have to be prioritised, usually because there is human need based on what has to be done. But I don't want to let others or myself down by doing such a bad job that I might as well not have bothered.

Which brings me to the germ of this post. For some reason, I've been asked a few times about energy *work* – using energy for ritual purpose, perception and tangibility of auras, that sort of thing. And without going into the argument about the reality of such, let's all agree to understand that *I* fully believe that energy exists. It's measured in terms of calories, fuelled by many different sources, and is clearly tangible in fire, light, heat etc. We use personal energy to keep us going. The limits of it haven't really been adequately assessed yet, but I'm sure that science will keep on investigating.

Metaphysically, there are many ways we can *feel* energy, both our own and that of others. It can be stolen. It can be transferred. But ultimately, you're using your own energy to do whatever it is you need to be doing. All of us, without truly intending to, give a lot of it away unnecessarily.

Case in point. I drove home today worrying virtually all the way about a harangue I had been on the end of from an irate person right before my shift ended. That person was cross and worried; I was on the receiving end. Nothing personal, but I genuinely had been trying to do my best and my efforts were constantly rebuffed. So I dwelt on it, as I am wont to do. What could I have done better? Could I have said anything different that might have helped more? The conversation was over, done and rapidly vanishing into the geographical and temporal distance, but it was still going round in my head. I got home finally… exhausted.

Facebook is full of it. The right-wing tabloids are other easy examples. So much random energy, thrown around with little factual information to back it up, as we just kick off at those who provide a convenient target. Or we suffer and worry because of those who have kicked at us. Either way, little productive or creative result comes from such random energy storms – more often than not, just destruction and distress.

Life can be tiring, with too much to do, and not enough time, as we all know. But I've been striving to *make* time, to relax a little, reading and suchlike, trying not to worry about those tasks that I'm not doing at that precise minute. But I'm always aware of them. So tonight, I've completed a few, despite my frustrations from the day, because I know that by this little act of creativity, I'll end up smiling. Not least because of all the rewriting and reworking that you don't see going on, but because the sheer freedom of just indulging in the brain-to-fingers activity of sharing my thoughts – while working out exactly what it is that I'm thinking – keeps the inspiration flowing.

Today I was sent a beautiful book by a first-time author, created with love and effort to inspire others. I'm now going to settle down with it and see what she has to say.

***

As I wrote this piece originally, it was just a tiny piece of writing on a very transitory medium, one web page amongst countless others. But now here it still is, in a real book, that I created. You're reading it – thank you.

In my turn, I am sending this book out into the world, a first-time author, created with the same manner and motivation as the one I read that night. And so the energy has been transformed into something worthwhile.

How is your energy being used? Are you fuelling yourself or others? Are you dragging everyone down with your own personal black cloud? We've all done it, there's no shame – but we can at least be aware. Nobody can be sweetness and light all the time.

Take a look at yourself, at your own energy. What does it feel like? How do you use it? How do others react to it? We're constantly changing, evolving (sorry Creationists)… how are we honouring the spirit that is *us*? Me, you, our families, friends, neighbours, and total strangers we might briefly interact with. Non-humans, animals and plants. Feel the different energies touching. What are you bringing to the dance?

Connection is at the heart of my Druidry as spirituality. Without awareness of that connection, we are closed off, sleep-walking, unfulfilled but constantly seeking the way to wake up. Just remember to feel, and feel others likewise (yes, absolutely, that snigger is entirely valid!). If we all did this, I like to think there'd be a lot less hurt being transferred across the world.

May your energies continue to fuel you and those you hold dear, as we are all held together.

Modern Mythologies

The common language of every human being throughout history is not English, Spanish or Cantonese. It is that of story. There are so many similarities between cultural myths, so many versions of fairytales – but with recognisable threads, instant familiarity. Told well, we are thrown back to our childhoods, automatically sitting to listen attentively to a tale well told, taking our own place within the tale as listener. What would we do if we were that hero? And that most basic of moral messages: what do we learn and take with us from the tale?

As Joseph Campbell taught, there are various story themes told again and again. Generally we follow a hero through trials and tribulations, as he defeats opposition and is rewarded with victory through his superior skills, which we can admire and emulate as we adventure through our own lives.

Stories reflect the age in which they are written. They carry the voices of our ancestors, and if they continue through the ages, chances are that they tell of human aspects that have not changed, issues that we face again and again, with suggestions on how to deal with them (or not). As with language, they reflect the culture in which they survive.

So then, to take an example close to my own home, who can name me a uniquely British mythological tale? I mean *British*, not those 'Celtic' tales so full of the energy of our close siblings the Irish, Scottish or Welsh. Something that captures the character of us here on this once-powerful isle. Something we will inevitably pass on to our own children.

King Arthur? Robin Hood? Any more...?

Those are good examples to start with, as alleged evidence of them still exists today in physical form: Tintagel, Glastonbury, Sherwood Forest, Nottingham Castle (albeit all very speculative or in entirely different form from the magical storybook versions). As a child, to find out that the places from the stories really *exist* brings them into a whole new dimension to the cartoon stories from America or Japan. These are places that you can really *visit!* The story becomes even more real.

A lot of British history has merged due to geographical boundaries changing, invasions and so forth, but these stories are as notable for their endurance as for the archaeological memories. They have changed through the ages as they were told, yes, but again, this reflects the tellers as much as the listeners. The British have been both, as they merge with those aforementioned siblings, and put their own stamp on other communities.

So, what's a modern British myth, something familiar to most folk here in the burgeoning twenty-first century? Sherlock Holmes, perhaps? Over a century old, but certainly showing his potential in the retelling. Or even that most timeless of fables, Doctor Who?

Now, I've had this discussion before and it's always met with laughter. But why not? I've heard Americans say (only half-joking) that they heard the British are made to watch this show from birth, learning it alongside the National Anthem. I don't *think* that's true.

Almost 50 years and still being told, this is a story that we are still creating, reflected differently for each generation. The Raggedy Doctor, the Wandering Angel, the madman, the clown. So much of humanity through the eyes of an alien, who loves humanity enough to help us. So are our tales reflected and retold.

(I am fully aware of the irony that it took the passion of a strong-minded team of Welsh creatives to bring this tale back to our lives this century, and that the current head writer is Scottish. But these are folk who never lost their storytelling skills, and are now (hopefully) showing us staid stiff-upper-lip-types how to imagine all over again.)

Recent tales demonstrate that the show's writers have an

excellent knowledge of traditional stories, spicing science fiction with popular images from classical mythology and tales of the land in which it is most often set. A peculiarly British eccentric (from his jelly babies to the restorative Cup of Tea), the Doctor travels through a land that we *know*, from council estate to Downing Street, allowing children to place the story easily into their world. We adults watching don't find it too difficult either.

So what does this have to do with Druidry? Aside from the travelling Bard being the one who sat at the fireside for a brief time, telling the story of adventures witnessed, heroes known and praised, villains castigated or humiliated, taking the listener far from the everyday to another world... and inspiring, shining a light on experiences that we never imagined, giving us something to truly aim for.

Has this ever been more needed?

The Doctor speaks. 'Do you know like we were saying, about the Earth revolving? It's like when you're a kid, the first time they tell you that the world is turning and you just can't quite believe it, cause everything looks like it's standing still. I can feel it... the turn of the Earth. The ground beneath our feet is spinning at a thousand miles an hour. The entire planet is hurtling around the sun at sixty seven thousand miles an hour. And I can feel it. We're falling through space, you and me, clinging to the skin of this tiny little world. And, if we let go...'[10]

We all have our stories, says the Doctor. 'In 900 years, I've never met anyone who wasn't important.'[11] So we learn to listen to those stories – to the tales each of us has to tell, that connect us as a community, as a species with shared experience. Although it's the Timelord as hero who draws us in, as with every story it's the humans in the narrative that we feel sympathy for, where we see ourselves reflected.

For one episode, the work of Dickens is given a new plot

twist, with the modern writer essentially stealing from the best to make something new, as Dickens himself did, and Shakespeare (another Doctor Who guest) before him. The entire production is focused on retelling a British story that calls to us, no matter who we are, here and now. We are entertained in the telling, but we are also learning and moving on. We feel a genuine joy in these stories that has been lost in a lot of modern 'entertainment,' and so it endures as we move forward.

The stories inspire us by telling *of* us, of our potential and the magic of life. The tale-tellers weave the words, but we are the ones left wondering how our own stories go, what they would sound like if told. And – if we truly are heroes in our own lives and learn to live well, as our stories merge with others – they may also be worth the retelling.

We inspire as we are inspired. Go forth and be fantastic in your story!

What's in a Name?

One of the Very Important Things that you Must Do to be a Proper Pagan (apparently) is Find Your Magical Name. Now, depending on who you read, you have your everyday name, your 'public' magical name, and your 'private' magical name, known only to you and your gods.

I could easily joke about this (specifically, my preferred reference point for such things being TS Eliot's poem, 'The Naming of Cats'). But I understand the meaning behind such thinking, and have been asked to address a specific question on the issue of names: 'Do you really need one? How do you pick/discover/find/get given one?'

In the late 1990s, I came up with 'Greycat' as a handy name on a Pagan forum as I started learning in earnest, seeing both the value in anonymity and getting a grin at the multifaceted simplicity of the image. I still do. Not black, nor white, but shades of grey – and that most curious and enigmatic of animals, from the house cat to the desert predator.

The name has stayed with me all these years later, now having merged with the everyday until this 'magical' name has become the same as the one I use to sign my cheques. While parallels can be drawn here between the special and the everyday (and how I'm murdering that difference by ignoring it), I fully recognise the need for a slight separateness when ritualising. Whether it be the robes, the tools or the name by which you refer to yourself, it's underlining that the work you are doing is of a certain type. All well and good; whatever helps to establish the frame of mind necessary to accomplish your goal.

I understand the importance of being called something that resonates with you. I considered this in some detail after my divorce – I now had the stages of my life mapped out in names, from maiden to marriage, through to where I am now. It makes for interesting times filling out security forms.

But how many of us have multiple names these days? Given names, by parents; internet 'handles'; nicknames; titles. Even 'Mum' or 'Dad'. What do you answer to? Who does that make you? How far do you identify with that collection of sounds?

It's when folk start referring to a 'true' name (which must, of course, be kept secret) that I start to twitch a little. Rather like those who refuse to let their tools be touched by anyone else, lest they 'contaminate' them with their energy. I do not, cannot and never have worked that way. Secrets will be broken sooner or later, objects will be touched – it is the nature of energy to be shared. Just look at quantum theory if you don't believe me. Names, of all things, are something that you use to refer to yourself – others must know it to use it, or it serves no purpose.

Now, I cannot tell anyone the ultimate secret of How to Find their Magical Name. Sorry. But I do believe in a) the Universe's deep and mysterious Sense of Humour and b) Synchronicity. Otherwise known as 'Pay Attention to Coincidence'.

Names come to us. If you've a particular reason behind seeking a new name (e.g. for magical work, or simply as a pseudonym) then you've probably already got an idea of which areas you're looking in. Animal, bird, magical creature... keep your eyes open and your mind aware, and something will pop up. It may have done so already and you've just not noticed.

Some take a name from their patron deity. Others choose aspects of the world that they feel suit them ('Hawkwind'). Occasionally a friend or working partner will say something that simply chimes 'right' to your ears. But, ultimately, can you imagine yourself saying to another person 'Hello, I'm Lady Moonbeam Riverdance'... does the name fit *you*? Can you stand before your trusted friends (let alone your gods) in truth and ask their opinion on your new moniker without being embarrassed or expecting gales of laughter?

I would advise keeping it simple. Also, a little research never goes amiss. A good friend of mine is a falconer by trade, and regularly annoys fair-weather pagans by asking who has 'Eagle' as a patron or name. He agrees that yes, the eagle is a proud, beautiful and noble-looking bird. Which, like many of its type, is a carrion bird with a relatively small brain. You pick the creature, you pick *all* of its aspects – expect them to manifest as you move forward with that association. Human definitions of 'cool' are not remotely universal, and you may not necessarily get what you bargained for. Be prepared to learn.

Which leads to the issue of realism. Practicality is one thing (calling yourself whatever you finally pick). But how well does it reflect *you*?

In this respect, it is not the 'true name' that you are seeking. It is a word that you are trying to best describe yourself, and the learning of that is the quest of a lifetime.

I'm not trying to put anyone off, or add more weight than is needed. While 'Huntingwolf Silverwillow' is all very well and good, I'd find that far too cumbersome, impractical and at heart, stupid. 'Cat' does me just fine. A name will be used for the serious and the silly; as I've said before, be prepared to laugh at yourself. There's not really any need to provide additional ammunition, your friends will do that – as my partner and I found when we were first referred to as 'Mog and Dog'.

These names will continue to refer to many aspects of us, with varying degrees of social acceptability, and new synchronicities as our lives progress. My name has grown on me, literally sticking as it reflects me – so the choice all those years ago was good. And I've certainly learned. After some work with my own darkness a few years ago, I remembered that the term 'cat' was shouted at me as a child more than once – as an insult.

What are you looking for in a name? What is its function, what do you need it to do? And does it reflect you *now*? OK – give it a try, see how it sits. Then try with those you work with… and branch outwards.

Life is about finding who you are. Let's see how your name fits that – and how others add their own tones to it likewise. You never know what you'll find, but keep moving forward.

You'll still be you, by whatever name.

A Pagan by Any Other Name...

Digging a little deeper into the topic (and mythology) of names, it has been suggested to me that by finding the 'right' name – your *true* name – you'll be able to somehow find your true self.

Now, most of us will be familiar with the idea that if you know a person's true name (and not necessarily a human person, but *everything* in creation), you will know their true self and be able to control them. It's familiar in folklore and fairytales throughout the world, with magical creatures somehow having innate knowledge of their own 'true' name, but with the rest of us left to muddle on with what our parents gave us.

Now aside from the issue of power and control, I find it a little hard to understand how one single word (even a convoluted and hard-to-guess word, such as the now-pretty-famous 'Rumpelstiltskin') can sum up everything that we are. No matter how long your life, from creation to destruction – and applicable to *everything*, from mayflies to mountains – that one word is you. Done. There you are, nicely labelled. And... err... you've decided your name is 'Lady Moonbeam Riverdance'...

I think this may be more an issue of labelling. As humans, we find it hard to take in complex concepts easily (especially in these days of information overload combined with short attention span). We need to box things up neatly.

I was asked once by a radio producer: "What should we announce you as?" The DJ knew me well, and usually just said 'Cat, Druid Priestess' or some such. This week, I was 'Cat, from The Druid Network and *also* the Ambulance Service!' Name, voluntary job and paid job. That's me, in a nutshell. Except, of course, it isn't – but it was most relevant to the discussion we were about to have.

Look at how you are called. First name, surname, title (Dr, Father), honorifics (Sir), nicknames, pseudonyms. Then consider who calls you what? Your boss won't call you 'Dad', but your child wouldn't call you by your surname.

Consider the tone of each, what each carries with it, what it means, what it feels like. How do you feel when each variation is used? Do you sit up straighter when called 'Sir' (especially by a policeman through a car window), do you automatically smile and relax when you hear 'Oi, Smithy!' Most parents I know both smile and roll their eyes at the plaintive 'Muuuuuuum'...

So which is most accurate? Or are they all? And ultimately – what do you call *yourself?* Do you prefer David to Dave? Do you know the original meaning of your given name? Who do you hold within your family name – the line of your parents, your husband, or someone else entirely?

And *then* come the labels. 'Priestess', 'Pagan', 'Druid', 'British'. And so on.

Your choices speak volumes about you in that brief moment – and *that* is the power of the words, the magic in the name that you're looking for. The associations built up around those simple syllables, so that when you are mentioned, the listener automatically has a picture in their mind, both the physical reality and everything else they tacitly know about you. This is why it's difficult when someone changes name – those powerful ingrained associations change with it.

In the UK, we were recently asked to complete the latest Census, our modern version of The Domesday Book (and now possible to complete online). There were mutterings about this, mainly about privacy, but also the difficulty of summing up an entire life in a series of tick-boxes and categorisations.

Yes, it grates a little that we're asked as a population to sum ourselves up in such a manner. It smacks of being 'just a number' to be counted, a tiny piece of data amongst millions. Although... that *is* what we are, to a greater or lesser extent. By filling in that form with our information, we are taking an active role in that community *as* who we are. That's the balance of living as unique people in such a wide and varied community, and the challenge of accepting the corresponding multitude of beliefs and lifestyles around us every day.

A question asked at many public-sector job interviews nowadays is: 'How do you define equality?' The *wrong* answer is: 'I treat everybody the same.' The *correct* answer is something along the lines of: 'I believe that everyone has an equal right to treatment and respect, but all have to be dealt with according to their individual needs.'

Think about that. While it's something we do every day, how difficult is it to truly treat everyone as individuals (regardless of your own beliefs)? What an enormous concept that is to grasp. Labels are *essential*… but must, ultimately, be flexible as we change and evolve in our busy and varied lives.

No matter what name you finally choose for your pagan work, once you start telling it to people, it's out of your control. You may have one idea of how it reflects your 'true self', but others will wrap it up with their ideas about you as a complete package. Basically, therefore, it's not just the name – it's the associations that go with it. How are *you*, as a Pagan/Druid/Heathen/Fairy Shaman representing *yourself?*

As Druidry has grown into a more publicly-acceptable and valid spiritual path, attitudes have changed. They will continue to do so as people learn more about what Druidry is. The associations around the label are changing. I'm contributing to that right now, with the information contained in this book, and in my daily life.

As a result, I'm often challenged on who I am, what I am, and how I am to be called. I have a certain image of myself, of course, but am also aware that others have theirs. Every time I prepare for a public rite, I'm nervous – always with the focus on doing my absolute best for those I'm acting for, but also because, as I said, I have no way of controlling how those present will perceive and understand me or what I'm doing. But every step adds to that knowledge – from that first glimpse of the robed woman walking barefoot across the grass, to the simple 'Hello' and smile. Labels are being adjusted, boxes becoming more pliable in that moment.

All I can do is remember that I am *me*. No matter the perception, I'm here and doing what I do. So are you. We *all* do our best to be ourselves. While the name is just a tiny part of that, of course it's important – but it's not the final truth about who you are: you're walking that every day. And twee though it may sound, there *is* no one quite like you.

What are you bringing to the world, to your name? How is your voice heard? What associations do you leave behind?

We stand huddled together against the cold, a huge pile of wood before us, lit branch in one man's hand, ready for the fire. It's a freezing winter night, but the rain has held off. Every one of us is eagerly anticipating the warmth of the impending blaze, preparing for the start of the ritual.

With some ceremony, the brand is thrown forward onto the pyre. We all breathe in expectantly.

Nothing happens.

Matches are brought out, but the wind puts paid to that. A small Zippo lighter is found – thank goodness for wearing street clothes under robes! But still the wood refuses to catch.

Someone runs off to fetch some lighter fuel. Still no effect. By now, the cold is seeping into our bones and frustration is starting to set in.

Suddenly, the wood bursts into flame! Sap crackles and a huge cloud of smoke billows into the night sky.

There's a small yell from the other side of the bonfire, and our cheers of success are effectively quenched by panic – is someone hurt?!

Nope. It was a yell of surprise, it turns out. Unsurprising, as we'd all just about given up.

Someone cracks a joke. We start giggling. No solemn ritual this, we've been made to work for it by the elements. But the nervousness and tension are gone, we're joined as a group, glad of each other's company finally having achieved that most basic of human needs: fire.

We warm ourselves and are grateful. And by the end of the evening, have laughed ourselves hoarse.

Just a Fool...

Every year, we have the time of April Fools. So let's take a look at that fellow who's friend to (and within) us all: the Fool.

As we wake up into Spring, the clocks change, the weather starts to brighten... and we all feel it within. March madness is traditionally depicted by the hare, but it does seem to be one of those periods when our connection to the land is most clearly felt. The sap is rising, we're able to cast off our winter coats a little, the old year is long gone – there's the sense of wanting to get out there after the hibernation time and just *do things!* (Yes, including *that,* but Beltane's only a month away – be patient!)

While our journey more truly started deep in the heart of winter, with the potential of ideas and gestation of thoughts, we're now in the Planting season. Ideas are being cemented more deeply, plans being acted upon with an eye to their harvest later in the year... or we're just having fun playing in the Spring sunshine (and rain!).

The first step on any journey is shown by the Fool in the traditional Tarot deck – because, in case you didn't know, we're all Fools when we start out: enthusiastic, full of energy, keen to explore wherever our feet take us... and about to fall flat on our faces along the way.

Taking a look at the image of the Fool in the Druidcraft Tarot deck, we see this beautifully depicted. The Fool is happily setting off on his or her journey, blue sky above, grassy field beneath. About to step off a cliff.

Now there are many sources of information about the Tarot out there, so I won't go into that too deeply here. But I have often been told that the best way to view the cards is to simply *look* at them and see what's there, how it applies to your situation. So here we are: where is the Fool for us as his day rolls around?

The Fool has everything he needs in his bag on his back, full of potential and energy, a smile on his face and a song in his heart. Being able to go barefoot in the grass is a real treat at this time of year, feeling plants growing in the earth again after the hard frosts and snow.

But what caught my eye in this particular card is the animal running alongside. A happy companion, perhaps? A black dog. The imminent fall ahead, the challenge beside... the Fool's journey is not going to be all flowers and sunshine.

April Fool's Day is a time of fun (depending on the level of the jokes being played!), but this is also a time when we really have to gird our loins and set off into the activity of the year. Planning should have been done, now the journey starts. No, we won't be entirely ready, but it's time to *move*.

Are we ready for the unseen pitfalls, the challenges that we will face? We have everything we need, remember, even if it's hidden deep down in the bottom of our pack. Are we able to maintain the excitement of the journey's start when the road starts to get rough or the bag starts to get too heavy?

For many Pagans, April Fool's Day has been adopted as the specific festival day of that most famous of tricksters, Loki. A shape-shifter in story, this fine gentleman is a cause of much dissent and discussion (and swearing) amongst modern-day pagans, due to his sheer complexity. But as I've said before, saying a deity is simply 'good' or 'evil' is far too simplistic – the very point of Loki is that he is never quite who he appears to be.

While not exactly as shown in the Tarot, Loki could easily be compared to the Shakespearean version of the Fool. He enjoys life, tearing headlong into scrapes before using his wits to extricate himself and those who inadvertently got pulled along with his enthusiasm. He manages to cut through the bullsh*t to the truth beneath. But notably, he expresses the full journey of life experience in his own tale as realistic rather than fantastic or idealised – from the initial excitement of exploring ('I wonder what would happen if I do *this...*') to the 'Oops' moment as things don't go entirely according to plan, and the resulting consequences. Like it or not, life does *not* end 'happily ever after' – you reap what you sow, and your actions *will* come back to haunt you. Sometimes with bells on.

Loki stands ready with a bucket of cold water, ready to throw it in your face. He deflates the pompous ass, screams 'WAKE UP!' when needed, or reminds you why standing on top of a hill in a suit of armour shouting 'All Gods are Bastards' is a bad idea (with thanks to author Sir Terry Pratchett).

I've had one Wiccan lady tell me flat out that Loki is a 'bastard son-killer' and refuse to have anything to do with him. Good luck, love – that's a challenge, right there.

Evil? Perhaps, but only when pushed too far (because every story needs a villain – it's just that this one refuses to remain two-dimensional). 'Morally questionable' might be more appropriate. But as with the Fool on his journey, it's more an exposure of what's inside us all, those parts we want to keep hidden brought out into the light to trip us up. We are made to face our challenges as they run alongside. That's part of the journey. We are no longer taught ethics in school, but as active pagans, it is necessary to constantly question – and we have deities such as this to 'help' us along.

In our nice, staid and organised Britishness, perhaps we've become a little scared of the Fool, of admitting that we don't know everything and might look stupid if we're caught taking a wrong step. But we don't, and we will – it's inevitable. That's the point where we pick ourselves up, take stock and move forward again; while now having learned not to take everything the strange red-haired man tells you at face value.

If you don't believe me, look up the story of the theft of Thor's hammer, and how Loki both caused and solved that Norse adventure. We need to laugh at ourselves – sometimes that's the only way to solve a problem. Sometimes that's the challenge itself.

This is why we honour the Fool: because he's there in all of us. Personally, rather than warding against the Fool (a path to failure if I ever saw one), I'd suggest investigating a little deeper. Once you get to your Fool, you'll see why he's survived so well all these years, despite having taken more knocks than Wile E. Coyote.

And this is why he's a very good companion to have with you as you journey forward.

Blessings of the Spring, sunshine and rain – may your cushions bring much whoopee…!

Curiosity or Satisfaction?

As part of my original training period years ago, my fellow students and I undertook the challenge of living with as much awareness as we could. Honourably living our daily lives with intention and curiosity, investigating our daily mundane rituals and habits – and then changing them as a result of what we found.

One comment that amused me recently was a work colleague saying that she would love to see how I live at home: "It must be really interesting!" So, I pondered, how do I live? What seems normal to me probably *would* be fascinating to others (hence the rise of reality television). But how much have I lapsed in my living, taking the easy way because of laziness, allowing myself to fall back into the automaton-like sleep of the commuter?

Reading the posts on pagan multimedia messaging boards seems to indicate how living in this particular faith is being very easily misinterpreted by the ingrained ways of our Western culture. 'I MUST HAVE this pentagram!' 'I can't afford the incense and candles for a ritual, what should I do?' Paganism as commodity, religion as shiny tools and bright jewellery. Without *this* item, the rite won't work properly. Compare this to the rich girls on MTV who delight in being filmed demanding ever-increasing luxuries, without which their lives won't be complete. No guilt or shame, because they have no sense that there is anything wrong with such a demanding nature.

I attended a national Pagan festival where a lady Wiccan was also giving a talk (dressed in flowing purple velvet, glitter and pointed witch's hat). "'Of course, you don't need all these tools to perform a ritual... but if you *do* want them, you'll find them on my stall downstairs.'" Integrity? Honour? Or making a living? Very little on her stall was made by her own hands.

I've heard a full-time shamanic practitioner in America state her anger at those who have approached her expecting training, but offering nothing in return. Not money, not food, not even a bit of help around the house. But they wanted a full shamanic apprenticeship. What were they expecting? Why were they asking?

Some newcomers to paganism (of any path) seem to think that spirituality can be bought. The instructions come within thousands of pages of instruction books, or on websites that contradict each other and change with the wind. 'Rare' artefacts are readily available (for a price) to help a seeker's vague goal – 'enlightenment', 'peace', 'power' – desperately sought without any true knowledge of what is being asked. Such a quest will never end, because such 'quick fixes' do not exist.

Is this not how we live, though? The next shiny gadget will make us happy. We've all done it – I've played with iPads in the electronics store, impressed with the futuristic simplicity of it, but with no way of ever affording one. It's fascinating to explore more deeply, to see the advancing technology and how it affects people. I've suggested that Apple has somehow tapped into the original source of desirability, as all of its products seem to draw the customer more effectively than other brands. Or it could just be that they're very well made and meet a common need.

On the positive side, such commercial development certainly raises the game for competitors and investigative research – but it's by no means accessible to all, without accumulating considerable personal debt. Hence the current financial difficulties faced by the Western world, desperate for goods beyond its means.

I have an ebook reader. I love it. A voracious bookworm, it certainly won't stop me buying those gloriously tactile paper creations. But, on consideration, which is more environmentally-friendly? The book-making process (wood pulp, processing, ink etc) or the plastic and metal within the reading device? The lights needed to read by, the power required to recharge... and ultimately, the words of the author. I am glad the stories continue to be told, by whatever medium. I will listen, and I will tell my own in turn.

We are connected to everything in life that we own, covet or touch. *Everything*. Our coffee in the morning was grown, harvested, ground, shipped and sold. The sugar and tea likewise. The milk probably came from miles away (despite the herd of cows in the field up the road from my house). I have a hybrid car – but still have to fill it with petrol. The plastic and glass that make my reading glasses. The fabric of my clothes. The bricks of my house. I may have bought it, but so many other hands have touched each item along the way – do I honour those shapers, makers and builders? Or do I ignore them in the rush to make something 'mine'?

The co-worker who asked about how I live was worrying, because she could not afford to buy food for the week... because her wages had been spent on a tattoo, make-up and shoes.

Please let me state: I am not attempting to guilt anyone into giving up everything and living as a hermit. We are each part of our own society. But within that, I am sadly drawing the conclusion that we have lost perspective on what is valuable. Value is placed on things rather than experience and relationship with those around (both human and non-human).

As a Druid, in awareness of my relationship to the world around as an indelible part of my faith, I endeavour to live as honourably as possible, so that I might stand in the knowledge of how my life affects and is affected by the efforts of others. This is not an issue of superiority, and I am not wishing to dictate or evangelise. I am simply asking for greater awareness.

I am glad that I have retained the urge to still be curious, to know how the things I use every day were crafted and where. Remembering with each touch to be thankful – that Fairtrade Guatemalan coffee, the unbleached sugar, the local milk. My meat and vegetables from a farm five miles away. Shopping in awareness. Will what I buy nourish me, or just be a quick fix that leaves only emptiness? This *can* be done quite easily – the cost of a fast-food burger meal would buy a small packet of farm-shop burgers, a sack of potatoes and bread fixings. It would feed more, for longer, and be infinitely more tasty and nourishing.

I can name those who hand crafted the (minimal) jewellery I wear, and am proud to support them. My ritual tools likewise. My candles from local hives. Ritual (and daily) bread with flour from a local mill. Keeping the relationship with the goods that I use and those who made them.

At work, my own wage is from public money (a considerable drop from the private-sector bonuses that I used to receive), but enough to live on and pay my bills. I do my best in my job, to provide the service expected and go that extra distance – as I do as priest. I do what is needed, and am grateful when others do likewise.

However, as I said, life is changing. Despite doing a good job professionally, work has not always been forthcoming due to that same difficult financial climate. But in the meantime, I have been preparing public rites around the country, working as a volunteer, holding workshops, visiting those who need both a friend and a priest... and writing this book.

Priorities are changing. What will I have to give up as a result? What do I really need? What can I afford, and what nourishes my family?

I will continue to question, to do my best to live with honour. To those around, to my Lord and Lady, family and friends. To all of you who read my words. To those unknown, but who still form part of my life.

Onward.

A Connection is Made

At Beltane 2011, my partner and I had the privilege of officiating a dual handfasting rite at Stonehenge, within the stone circle at sunset.

Every single public rite I have performed has held its own special place and importance, each raising the bar for me in a new (and often terrifying!) way – but such is the challenge of the role I have undertaken. My own promises are constantly tested. I do my best for every single individual who asks.

The significance and impact of this particular site, of course, cannot be underestimated. As I drove South, I was constantly reminded of an image, not from the mainstream Pagan literature, but from Mark Chadbourn's wonderful books, the 'Age of Misrule': lines of blue fire run across the land, converging at key points to produce a special effect on those who can tap into it. Obviously a reference to ley line theory, but the sense of impending ritual that began for me as I set off on such a journey was almost tangible. The sheer *oomph* of the site is indisputable, and must be recognised and respected.

That week, however, those involved started talking about a particular effect of the rite we had not foreseen. Increased connection to the land, to the Powers That Be, to the Pagan path, for a call to practise. Whether it be the ritual itself, the location, the impact of the promises made or a combination of all, from those who were just entering the world of 'real' Pagans to those who had been walking the path for some years, an impact was clearly being felt. I'm very glad to say that I've seen it continue, in an extremely positive way for all concerned. Wonderful to witness.

In fact, I'd heard of this phenomenon before. Life is tough, there's no denying, and it's easy to get bogged down in the stresses of the everyday. When time is taken to make a special journey – be it general holiday or specific pilgrimage – to a site of significance, a 'recharge' is often spoken of as a result. I've felt it myself: the 'feel' of a certain area brings a bubbling up of emotion. Blocks are broken down, joy wells up. From the spectacle of the landscape (Glastonbury Tor) to the sheer feeling of the land under your feet (Salisbury Plain), there's a definite difference to the feeling that you get when walking down a normal high street.

Now I'm not going to go into ley line theory here. Since my archaeological studies back in college, I've been intrigued by such ideas, but whether there is some intrinsic power in the land reaching beyond humanity, or the power is triggered by our beliefs themselves and the associations we give to it, each experience is ultimately subjective. I'd rather hear your stories than possible academic explanations (although those do, of course, fit into the overall mythic web).

But I'm thinking we might well be fooling ourselves to some degree. While certain sites may be the equivalent of cosmic energy substations, where we can 'plug into' the energy of the land to give ourselves a boost, that in itself seems a little simplistic. England is a big place. The idea of geographical focal points seems a very human one, in the same vein as requiring specific tools to perform a rite for how they make us feel rather than their physical necessity. Why are some sites more intrinsically 'magical' than others? Why then do different places get very different reactions from those of different faiths? How much does our belief *make* the magic, versus tangible reality?

'But can't you just wave your hand and make all the dirt fly away, then?'

'That works,' said Tiffany, 'but only if you wave them about on the floor with a scrubbing brush.[12]'

For a rite as important as a handfasting, the location is an important component of the rite. The couple will choose it in the same manner as they choose what they will wear, the paraphernalia on the altar, those they will invoke or thank. But all of these must serve an active purpose. Certainly 'spectacle' is a purpose – but I've performed a handfasting on a golf course in the Midlands, and it was no less wonderful than any other!

Intention is what brings the rite together. The sense of connection should come about because of that shared focus and aim, both between the people directly involved and those present in spirit. All are honoured and acknowledged, and so jointly add to the energy brought to bear, both visually and in other, deeper ways.

But we don't experience handfastings (or any other major public ritual) every day. So how do we stop ourselves sinking into the morass of mundanity that challenges us daily? How do we maintain that connection when away from the 'special' places and the 'special' clothes?

The land is still there, beneath our feet. The sky is above. The air is around. That blue fire runs through each and every one of us. The difficulty comes in remembering and recognising that, acknowledging it and calling upon it when needed, to reaffirm the connection that is, in fact, *constantly* present. Even (especially) if subsumed by concrete.

As I've mentioned before, each place has its spirits, its own mood, which influences us both knowingly and subconsciously. 'Ugh, I hate going to [insert place name here], it's horrible, just grey and nasty.' 'Oh, I love [insert place name here], it's so beautiful, it feels really nice and peaceful.'

How do our own places feel? Where we live immediately, and in wider circles reaching out? You may not like your town, but how does your home feel amid that – subsumed by the negative, or a small oasis of calm just for you? Or the opposite: a lovely city around, but home life as a pit of despair from which you try your best to escape? How do you affect that?

I do speak from experience. When the day is a bad one and I'm overwhelmed with black thoughts, my connection is also blocked – possibly for my own sake, as my mind panics and pulls the blinds down and the shields up – but sadly, that is the worst course of action for improving the situation. Opening up may seem almost impossible sometimes, for the sake of what might flood out as well as in, but like it or not we are part of the world around. We connect, we learn... and we remember who we are, and how to heal.

I've stood in the middle of London (and Brighton, Nottingham or Newcastle), often described as a morass of surging humanity that easily overwhelms any who can't withstand it. A lot of city-dwellers act accordingly – just look at their faces. They're oblivious to what's around, blocking it for their own sake, but suffering even more as a result of missing so much. The difficulty is accepting, opening up to what's there. Modern cities *are* huge, with so much going on... but brace yourself if you can, and take a look. How does it feel? How are you part of it by the very act of standing there? Now can you see the others whose minds and spirits are truly awake?

While a constant challenge, this is the path that I walk. Forgetting or blocking the connections that exist around is detrimental to my own well-being, but this also prevents me from fully *seeing* what's around – and is pretty disrespectful to those trying to assist. While some well-meaning friends may be unbearable in a time of crisis, others understand and simply listen. Those (not necessarily human) companions are good for that. They don't judge, but simply offer perspective.

I'm not *more* connected than anyone else, by any means. I simply practise, as I've been trained (and still have to be reminded) to do. I should probably know better by now than to block myself – and I still get my rear kicked as a result on both a real and cosmic level – but life *is* hard. While the beauty and power of a certain place will always buoy us up, we must do our best to remember that we're never really alone, and we have the ability to make things brighter and more magical. It's maintaining the relationship with what's around us that's the trick.

Open eyes, dig roots deep, feel what's around. Where are you, and what are you doing?

Open or Closed

Another question:

'It can be hard sometimes to keep in tune with energies, especially when life is going through a rough patch. How do you keep yourself open?'

Is this the $64,000 question for spiritual seekers? How do we keep awake, aware and listening, just in case we miss something – a call from the gods, a sign of where to go, some crucial bit of information without which we are stuck in our rut of normality...

I do understand, of course. Brought up in the society of the Western world today, perhaps it is true to say that a large part of our search for 'something better' is due to how much modern society does *not* provide answers, motivations, or much beyond persistent bad news and advertising. Thanks to the media, authority figures are now emperors disrobed. Traditional religion is either discarded or disregarded, politics corrupt or so far removed from each of us as to be irrelevant. At worst, we are out of control of our lives, working hard to make money that appears to be decreasing in value compared to the goods we need, with constant dissatisfaction leading us to medication and reality television...

Except it's not like this, not in so simplistic a form. Certain newspapers would have us think so, and it's always easier to whinge than to rebel or challenge the perceived status quo. But life has always been difficult. Humanity has looked to faith (religious, secular or scientific) to provide answers, but is now challenging those findings – and complaining that they do not provide. Adults are living like children, expecting that demands will be easily fulfilled and complaining (to the extent of legal action) when this does not happen.

But there are always those who question and act. One

blessing of mass information is that individuals are starting to realise that outwardly with the economic crisis, and internally with the constant quest for a happy standard of living for ourselves and our families, we need to look more deeply for solutions. Why are things happening in this way? How can we change things for the better? Entire societies are being overthrown because so many people have had enough.

There is also awareness that a one-size-fits-all policy cannot work for everyone. If we want to be recognised as individuals, we must also realise that we are individuals making up a society. We will not be catered to exclusively – we must play our part.

From a pagan perspective, this makes for interesting times. One attraction of Paganism (whichever path) is that you are your own priest. You need no third-party individual to speak to the gods on your behalf – you can do it yourself. Hurrah!

Except… it could be argued that has always been the case. Every person, of every faith, has at some point said 'Oh God, help me'. Conversations with deity are encouraged. It's those who choose to follow the priest's vocation who took it upon themselves to dictate public or mass practice, according to their own interpretation.

Which is, to some extent, what I'm doing here. I'm not telling anyone how to live their lives – but I've taken it upon myself to act as priest in public, so to some extent, am providing that third-party mediation. And this *is* needed. People come to me asking, so I try to provide. Why would this be the case, if we are all our own priests?

Because while we are individuals, with our own ideas, lives and needs, we need community. Be it our immediate physical neighbours, close friends, family or Twitter followers, we exist in relation to others. Sometimes those individuals have more experience, greater specialist knowledge, or just an alternate perspective that will help us understand our own problems a little better.

The priest's function is to serve, both themselves and others. One joy of modern paganism is that this is recognised: the priest does not exist on a pedestal, but lives their own life, available for a chat, fully happy to be questioned, able to admit their own questions and seek answers together with those they work with. Not everyone will agree with each other, but that leads to greater understanding of combined individual versus group needs. New ideas, greater cohesion, varied perspective.

To return to the original question, then – how to remain open in times of trouble? Connect. You probably guessed I'd say that, but I mean it.

Yes, certainly, please do go outside and sit with your patrons, deities, ancestors, local spirits, pets or garden. But don't remain isolated in your practice if you have good friends who can help *as well.*

It can be hard, but opening to the world around means opening up to other people, rather than staying stuck in your own head. Share ideas. Putting very subjective spiritual experiences into words is a challenge, but it helps you to get things straight – and usually experience an 'Aha!' light-bulb moment of realisation along the way. You'll see synchronicities. Others may well have experienced similar things. You can move forward together, reassured and reinforced, making practical and effective change. Your friends can also point out something that might have been under your nose all along – but that you just couldn't see for looking.

Obviously, as I've said before, 'regular' friends may have a very different worldview to your own, requiring a more gentle approach to such a discussion. Approach those whose perspective you value, that you know will listen sympathetically. But remember that you may be required to speak and explain so as to create understanding, rather than just blurting out what's on your mind. When the questions come, that's when you may begin to realise that there's more than just your own perspective

– your workmate will have a different idea of you than your parents or siblings, and this will influence their suggestions as to what action to take. All are valuable, all add to the mix, but it's ultimately up to you what you do next.

As workers with what has been called 'subtle reality', most Pagan practitioners have a sense of the energies of ourselves and others (human and non-human), as well as how some work together and others clash. With practice, when 'open', we can actually perceive the discordant notes, question them, discover flaws, fix problems… or simply notice a different outlook that changes us in turn.

There will always be people older than you, more experienced in certain aspects of life, but not necessarily having experienced anything in exactly the same manner as you. You bring your own subtle shading to the greater picture, and blending with others helps you to realise that you are just one small individual and yet also a far greater power than you might have originally thought.

Sooner or later, someone will come asking you for help in turn. Do you step up, or scuttle away to hide? What are you bringing to the pagan picture? You've made the commitment to practise – now's the time to realise that being 'open' is a constant process. Move forward at your own pace, but *do* move forward. Be prepared to be questioned, but question yourself likewise. Challenge, build trust, fall down, get up. That's life.

Being open is being an active participant. So, back to my favourite question: *What are you doing?*

What is Community?[13]

The idea of 'community' has changed dramatically in recent years. Quite a few of us are more comfortable in online groups, communicating via email and social networks, as they give us the freedom to chat when and where we like. Our friends are scattered far beyond our regular everyday boundaries, and the world opens up for us to touch at a keystroke.

It would clearly be hypocritical of me to denigrate this 21st-century mode of relationship, since I'm regularly in touch with friends as far away as Taiwan or as 'local' as the next town, all from the personal space of my chair and laptop. By the creation of my own blog, I've grown to meet and correspond with other writers around the world, seeing the wider Pagan community through the creative output of single individuals all working together — a truly marvellous thing, that has never before been possible. Technology has allowed instant community.

Last summer, I went on retreat to a Druid Camp in Lancashire: 'the Flame of Brigantia'. It was a small gathering of around 30 people, adults and children, families, couples and individuals. Some were already friends, but the group was mostly made up of strangers — some even strangers to the Druid path. All brave (or foolish!) enough to drive into the remote hills and moors simply to meet other like-minded folk… and inadvertently delve a little deeper into their own Paganism.

Nobody was really sure what would happen, but all were friendly and willing. Many will be keeping in touch via computer now that we have all gone back to our separate homes, but the memory of time together is strong — already people are looking forward to meeting up again.

This Camp was set up via a website, advertised via the internet and social networks, but came together in a very real and magical weekend. Relationships were formed and strengthened by it, and will no doubt continue to grow until/if we do meet again.

As a more public, active Druid in the community, I was casually asked whether I was a member of a Grove. I had to stop and think — am I?

(I'm tempted to explain that for those who don't know, a Grove is to Druids what a Coven is to Witches — just with more trees. But I think you can work it out.)

I've been a member of a Grove in my local community, meeting in the woods every month to work together and solve the problems of the universe (as does any good social group). But the busy-ness of modern life — family, distance, time, money, transport — caused it to fracture. I still talk to each and every other person from it, and have no doubt that if it were revived, many would do their best to be there. But meantime, what is my 'Grove?' What is my Druid Community?

Is it the international charity of which I am trustee and volunteer? Is it the local regional group that I help with when called upon? Is it one of any number of social media groups, internet forums, blog rolls or suchlike that I contribute to when the muse takes me?

Or is it those I speak to regularly, discussing their spirituality, problems and achievements, or just gossiping as friends? Whether in person in a café or at home, via telephone or instant messenger, or even text message — this is still real communication, with a real community. The close-knit group of friends that I call my own has grown a great deal in recent years, but I have promised that if needed, I will be there for them by whatever means they require — from helping to move house, to carrying an emergency kit in the car for late-night speeding down the motorway to a friend in dire need (yes, really).

This, I think, is where the virtual community meets the tangible. When you're having a bad day and feel the need to share that via a brief Tweet, you'll get support from online friends — even a brief 'hugs' message shows that folk are out there caring about you, hoping that you're OK. Sometimes more concrete support comes from those who can help with that specific issue. Wonderful! You've reached so many in just a few lines.

When real, tangible support is needed, however, what do you do? When madness looms, when the world is shaking from its safe axis of normality, who do you call? Family member, friend, priest? Not everyone has any of those. But for my own special community, I do my best to be as good as all three — from a cup of tea and a venting session, to a lift to the hospital, to a full-on ritual in their front room. I made my promise: if I can, I'll be there. If I can't, I will do what I can, whatever's best as needed.

I think a lot of modern folk are wont to forget the reality of community. You're an active part of it, responsible for your own actions within it and as a single brick that makes the foundation of the group that much stronger. Sometimes 'hugs' is fine; sometimes more is needed. We're learning this as we touch each other internationally, and it's a tremendous joy to me that so many rise to the challenge so magnificently.

From that personal touch in tangible reality, to a real letter of support for a total stranger on the other side of the world, we are a community. You may not be Druid; I may not be Wiccan. But we are all Pagan. We need to support each other in these exciting times, sharing our hopes and dreams and then working to make them real and visible.

In the world today, it may sadly not be realistic to form meaningful community with family or neighbours — one created by a twist of bloodline, the other by the dice-roll of finding a house. But soul-deep, heartfelt and evolving communities are now springing up more strongly than ever, growing and flourishing far beyond what could ever have been expected from traditional geographical groups. This is no bad thing. But it's still up to us to make them work.

So, my favourite question for fellow Pagan practitioners, as part of a community that encourages active responsibility: What Are You Doing?

Everybody Knows...

I've noticed that one of the most common conversation-starters to me is 'You're never going to believe this but...' or 'I'm *not* crazy but...'

When people find out that you may be even a little bit sympathetic or knowledgeable about the supernatural, the stories start flowing. Ghosts, strange experiences, things that you don't talk about as a matter of normal life for fear of being mocked, embarrassed or locked up in a room with rubber walls and crayons.

I recently heard some wonderful tales about a ghost kitten that plays with the living cats around a house, a ghost policeman who still performs his duties in what is now a domestic residence, the comparative effect of personal energy levels based on the weather, crystals or other people... call it what you will, there are things in this world that are currently unexplainable, but commonly felt.

I've never studied science formally past GCSE level, but have become fascinated with quantum theory and the effect of energies as we discover more and more about this great universe. I once asked an online science forum whether there were any studies of human energies (e.g. auric fields and suchlike) with a view to investigating how they can affect and be affected by their surroundings. Given that we clearly produce energy – by being living animals – the response that I received was rather surprising: 'Why bother, what's the point?' Basically, such theories would be 'bad science', and best left to the likes of Uri Geller.

And yet, the theory is clearly tacitly understood by most of us. The 'Matrix' movies openly suggest human bodies can be used as batteries. A unit of energy consumed and burned by every one of us every day is immediately familiar: the calorie. These are the same calories that can be quantified by burning any fuel; coal has a calorie content (bad news for those pregnant ladies out there).

One of the basic beginner lessons in most magic or energy work texts is the simple game of rubbing your hands together fast, then separating them while still remaining aware of the charge between your palms. Once you become more skilled, you can become able to sense (or even see) the energies of others, or direct focused energy yourself. Using a wand, a staff or even your finger, most of us have been 'zapped' at one time or another – hence grounding (as described previously) is a crucial beginner lesson.

Short of being nervous of the unknown, I am puzzled as to why so many feel such familiar actions or mysteries are *not* worthy of study – perhaps because the empirical scientific method may not be able to accurately assign meaning and category easily. Surely Jung's widely known theories of the collective unconscious are worth pursuing? If divination is bunkum, why is it still practised – is it a placebo or a psychological tool? There are still many things to be discovered about both the world around us and ourselves in relationship. Curiosity should be encouraged, not stifled!

As I said earlier, a lot of people simply want to tell me about their experiences, with a look in their eyes that shows the simple wish for understanding. They're not mad. They experienced something as real as a handshake, as solid as a wall, as visible and tangible as anything else around us. To be then told that this was somehow 'not valid, not real' is both disrespectful and, frankly, ignorant.

Why simply ignore another's story? Dismissing someone without listening, without even attempting to understand, degrades them and prevents you from possibly learning something new. Even if it's something so unusual, unfamiliar or frightening, I try my best to comprehend what they experienced, to listen to the tone beyond the words – why are they telling me?

Do they expect me to have an explanation (sometimes), or just wanting to be heard (more usually)?

Yes, sometimes judgement is impaired. Sometimes there is misdirection going on, misunderstanding or simply assigning the unusual to a basic activity for the sake of excitement or a 'wow' factor. But still, it can make a good story! Very few tales are utterly worthless; there is always a reason behind the telling, as well as the data involved. Is it worth exploring further? Maybe, maybe not – but we all know, inside, that everyone has experienced something unexplainable. It's whether they are brave enough to look deeper, or not. Even if you then find a simple mundane explanation, you've expanded your knowledge, and can investigate further into the possible origins of a superstition or myth.

If you're walking this path of modern Paganism, you'll have experienced so much unusual 'stuff' that it's probably not even unusual any more. That's the next level: realising that the 'supernatural' *isn't*. Even if we can't quantify it with statistics, what exists in nature is, by definition, natural. So our experience is immediately validated. Let's press on, try to see what this means.

When we move into the dark time of the year, people realise and react. We start to think about Halloween, ghost walks are held in town centres and the television is full of 'alternative' entertainment. Ultimately, we as society like a good story, and a ghost story around the camp fire is a tradition as old as humanity. We like to learn about living with the unexplained because we have to – there's not an easy answer to everything. The darkness hides many mysteries that tug at our ancient animal instincts.

As the scientist can explain the intricacies of a healing drug, the engineer the workings of technology, so the Druid, shaman or priest can help with the stranger side of life. Yes, it can be silly or funny to hear about a supernatural experience... but it can also be deeply disturbing. This is why most feel the need to share with a specialist. That is why they come up to me and nervously stammer: 'You'll probably think I'm nuts, but...'

No. I don't. I'll listen. And then we'll see what next. We move on together, explore, work with that connection.

Life is full of magic and mystery, and I wouldn't have it any other way. It's up to us what we make of it.

Keep exploring, friends. The fire's burning over here, if you want to come and sit awhile.

Honestly...

I've been told that I have a terrible poker face. It's often true. I suppose I can be described as naive. It's just that... well frankly, I get very confused by bullsh*t, and how naturally it comes to some people.

You know what I mean. The rubbish that some individuals (and groups) surround themselves with daily, whether it be out of ego, pride or just as armour to hide behind. They live their labels – designer or title. And it's just crap.

I've done it, because I had to. I lived in London for years, and it's practically a pre-requisite there. If you're honest in your actions and conversations, people stare, more used to buzz-words and trite small talk. It's a survival mechanism – the mask goes up, the stride is in place, you're untouchable and ready to walk down Oxford Street. You don't see everyone else, there's just you... because everyone else is doing the same (if you spot anyone actually looking about, they're a tourist). True friends are a rare and valuable commodity.

But as I've moved back into the natural world, the active, participatory and visible closeness of the countryside, I can be myself again. I learned to shrug off the mask with a laugh. If I felt the need to hide, to pin the smile on before I left the house, there was something wrong (which has been known).

Looking back, I first found this as a child. Happily bimbling about, discovering things, playing. Then – school. Where if you speak your truth, in blissful ignorance of what you *should* be saying according to some rule set that you never got, or some group that you were never 'cool' enough to join (because you didn't get that memo), you're laughed at, tormented. Adults smile gently and sigh, suggesting you might like to act a bit differently, to better fit in.

I was weird, obviously. I used to spend all available time

either mucking about in the trees around the playing fields, or buried in a book. My entire high school lunch period can be summed up in one word: *library*.

Teenagers, of course, all think they have the 'right' attitude, that certain knowledge of how to live. Some groups set the rules, others blindly crash about trying to conform to them; still others make a point of ignoring them, and thereby set their own. What's important? What's of value? What gets you through the day?

This carries through into adult life, sadly. While going into therapy (either clinical or via self-help books) to find their 'inner child', those smiles are plastered on for dinner parties, speaking to workmates and neighbours, keeping up a certain standard, an approved image. Even the psychology of 'finding yourself' has become a familiar phrase, over-used, over-simplistic and meaningless.

How cynical, this sit-com falseness. And, I have to ask myself, how really true?

I do come across people who complain of having to 'keep up appearances'. But at the same time, more and more folk are actually trying to break past the mask. They're actively seeking out a lifestyle that works for them, something that makes them happy; the life they want to lead that they've never been taught how to find, or permitted the freedom to look for. They're learning to laugh at the lies, before walking away.

This can involve battles – it's life. It can result in divorce, loss of material comforts, even loss of family. But how far do you have to go to strip back to yourself, to truly live honourably according to your own personal truth? And why is that so hard for others to grasp?

When I was moving out of London, I got envious looks, and bizarre plaudits: 'Wow, you're finally *getting out!*' 'I wish I could.' Well, why can't you? There are quite a few places outside the M25.

We trap *ourselves*. Or we inadvertently trap others, by our own fears and jealousies. Parents cling to children, partners to each other, friends to those who listen. But such neediness and false love often only serves to drive the other away. Not everyone does well in captivity, even if it's a gilded cage. It's not a relationship of balance; it's slavery, parasitical.

I'm glad to say that more and more often, I'm seeing folk listening to others for the honest joy of hearing what they have to say. Difference is celebrated, skills are praised and encouraged. Lies and conceit are punctured and laughed at. Titles and labels are questioned.

I've worked hard on my book. I've done my best to be honest, to speak my truth (it's not fiction, so why should I lie?). I'm telling a story, yes, but it's mine, and I'm striving to write accurately. I'm very aware that once it's out there, it's even more public than the moment when one version of these words was let loose across the internet. A book is more meaningful, more permanent. So I'd better be able to stand by what I say.

I've also put myself up to public questioning. My first full-day workshop was full of interested people travelling to hear what I had to say about Druidry. Me. I used to vomit before reading aloud in class, conduct university seminars while *in the throes* of a panic attack, be actively phobic of exposing myself to others in any way.

So what *is* Druidry? How *can* I call myself one? How true is it? How much do I honestly believe what I'm saying?

I promised myself that I would do my best.

I've spoken of the difficulty that we all have of expressing ourselves honestly, of stopping in the middle of a sentence that rings false, before taking a breath and starting again. How this might actually result in the respect of others (who might not have the strength to ever admit that they are wrong in their stories or decisions). My life has reached the stage where I actively *DO NOT WANT* to lie, to create a conceit, to live a label.

How easy would it be? 'Yes, I'm a Druid, don't you know. See my robe and staff!' Pfft. Any tools that don't serve a purpose have been dumped. My faith is not about how much Stuff I can accumulate, physically or in attitude.

But I have realised how closely the word 'Druid' equates to my personal beliefs, those felt in my heart and in my spirit. The love of the life in the world, the amazing variety presented every day: people, animals, plants, landscapes, seasons. The stories of others, the glow as they open up and truly laugh as they create honest connection. Simple amazement that someone is listening.

It shouldn't be so difficult to be yourself. But we're getting there, if we truly want to.

So this is my statement of Thanks.

Thank you to those who have listened to me, and are still listening. Those who love, laugh and try to make sense of both the darkness and the enthusiasm that pours from me (both fairly incoherent and confusing to the uninitiated!). Those who appreciate me for what and who I am, how my heart expresses itself and how my words sing my song. Those who haven't taken my honesty as foolishness, ignorance or an opportunity to take advantage.

To me, such a relationship is the greatest gift that there can be. I love and honour those of you who are honest with me.

May your lights shine brightly and inspire, as I know they will.

29th November 2011

I stride confidently on, through the dark tunnel, my partner keeping step on one side, staff striking the ground firmly on the other. Others follow us, but I'm only half aware of them. Much more is waiting.

I climb the gentle hill, feeling the soft grass underfoot, where so many have stepped before me. The wind blows hard around, stealing my breath, swirling my cloak dramatically. I move carefully, so as not to trip.

At last, my journey has brought me here. A combination of chances, unforeseen luck and considered decisions. I could never, ever have foreseen it unfolding like this.

The sun is setting. I must get on.

I pause... and step into the stone circle.

I cannot speak. The immensity of what is around, the weight of the land, those ancestors in blood and spirit, threatens to overwhelm me.

I look up and see faces, waiting expectantly. I nod and focus.

Be with me, my friends.

I move forward, carrying the past and shaping the future, to do what I must, what I am called for.

Onward, together.

Notes

1 'Everyday Magic', by Dorothy Morrison. Llewellyn Publications, 1998

2 'Dogma', dir. Kevin Smith (2008)

3 'Dogma', dir. Kevin Smith

4 'Quicksilver', by Neil Stephenson. Arrow, 2004

5 'Animism, Anarchy and Living Druidry', by Emma Restall Orr. Originally published in 'Sacred Hoop' (2004) – http://www.emmarestallorr.org/pdfs/AnimismAnarchy.pdf

6 'Earth Pilgrim', by Satish Kumar. Green Books Ltd, Devon, 2009

7 'My Booky Wook', by Russell Brand. Hodder, 2008

8 'Advanced Witchcraft', by Edain McCoy. Llewellyn Publications, 2004

9 'Neopagan Rites: A Guide to Creating Public Rituals That Work', by Isaac Bonewits. Llewellyn Publications, 2007

10 'Rose', Doctor Who episode by Russell T Davies. BBC, 2005

11 'A Christmas Carol', Doctor Who episode by Steven Moffat. BBC, 2010

12 'Wintersmith,' by Sir Terry Pratchett. Corgi Childrens, 2007

13 Originally published on 'The Pagan Household' website, July 19 2011

Moon Books, invites you to begin or deepen your encounter
with Paganism, in all its rich, creative, flourishing forms.